THE SERVANT GIRL PRINCESS

CARABOO

THE *REAL* STORY OF THE *GRAND* HOAX

JENNIFER RAISON

AND MICHAEL GOLDIE

<u>INTERLINK BOOKS</u>
An imprint of Interlink Publishing Group, Inc.
NEW YORK

First American edition published 1995 by

INTERLINK BOOKS
An imprint of Interlink Publishing Group, Inc.
99 Seventh Avenue
Brooklyn, New York 11215

Library of Congress Cataloging-in-Publication Data available

ISBN 1-56656-179-5

Printed and bound in Great Britain

Contents

Acknowledgements   vii
Authors' Note   ix

The Mystery

CHAPTER ONE   The Arrival   5
CHAPTER TWO   The Workhouse   9
CHAPTER THREE   Interest is Aroused   13
CHAPTER FOUR   An Unknown Language   19
CHAPTER FIVE   Life at Knole   23
CHAPTER SIX   In which the Manner of Caraboo's
                     Appearance in England is Discovered   29
CHAPTER SEVEN   Caraboo goes to Church   37
CHAPTER EIGHT   Caraboo is Painted and Dr Wilkinson
                     appears on the Scene   43
CHAPTER NINE   Caraboo's Disappearance and Illness   53
CHAPTER TEN   The Unmasking   67

The Confession

CHAPTER ELEVEN   I Embark Upon the World   85
CHAPTER TWELVE   I Become a Cook   93
CHAPTER THIRTEEN   I Fall Sick   99
CHAPTER FOURTEEN   The Jew's Wedding   109
CHAPTER FIFTEEN   The Magdalen   121
CHAPTER SIXTEEN   I Fall among Highwaymen   131
CHAPTER SEVENTEEN   I am Married   141

CHAPTER EIGHTEEN   My Son is Born   151
CHAPTER NINETEEN   My Time with the Gypsies   161

The Search for the 'Truth'

CHAPTER TWENTY   Captain Palmer Investigates   171
CHAPTER TWENTY-ONE   An Enigma to the End   185

Appendices   194
Notes   198

Acknowledgements

I am grateful to Hunter Steele, for showing me the style suitable for the 'Confessions', and to the Central Reference Library, City of Westminster, Central Library, Bristol, the Bodleian Library, Oxford, Shire County Records Office, Gloucester, the Wills Memorial Library, Bristol, and the Art Gallery, Bristol; also the library in Bath.

I have quoted where possible from original books and manuscripts. *Notes and Queries* and *The Gentleman's Magazine* from the relevant dates are on the open shelves in the British Museum Reading Room, and these have been most helpful for the flavour of the times.

AUTHORS' NOTE

Mrs Worrall's Journal and letters are an elaboration of the text. As far as possible we have attempted to reconstruct what might have happened around what actually did happen. J. M. Gutch, who published the story of Caraboo, and on whose text this book is based, was the editor of *The Journal*, under the pseudonym of 'Cosmo'.

Mr Worrall does not seem the same man Mrs Worrall mentions in her Journal and letters, but then many men have a public and a private face.

Mary's 'Confessions' exactly follow her movements prior to the hoax, as related to Mrs Worrall and Mr Mortimer. However far-fetched some of the incidents seem, they come in the main from Mary herself. Wherever possible, her actual words have been used.

THE MYSTERY

CARABOO

'On the third of April, 1817, the Overseer of the Poor of the Parish of Almondsbury, Gloucestershire, called at Knole Park, the residence of Mr Samuel Worrall, to inform that gentleman and his wife that a young female had entered a cottage in the village, and had made signs that she desired to sleep there – but NOT SPEAKING A LANGUAGE WHICH ANYONE UNDERSTOOD, he thought it right to refer to Mr Worrall as a county magistrate for his advice, there being also a manservant residing with his family who knew several foreign languages.

The female was, therefore, brought up to Knole mansion, but to which removal she showed signs of reluctance, and refused for some time to enter its doors.

At last she was prevailed upon to go in, and was presented to Mr and Mrs Worrall, who with their servant were unable to understand her language, but made signs to her to show any papers in her possession, when she produced a bad sixpence and a few halfpence, and implied that she had nothing else.

She had a small bundle with a few necessaries, and soap in a bit of linen.

Her dress was a black stuff gown with a muslin frill round her neck, a black cotton shawl on her head, and a red and black shawl round her shoulders, tastefully put on in Asiatic style. The general impression from her person and manners was attractive and prepossessing. Her head was small, her eyes and hair black, forehead low, nose short, complexion a brunette, her cheeks tinged with red, mouth rather wide, white teeth, lips large and full, small round chin, height about 5ft 2in. Her hands appeared unused to labour, and her age about 25.'

Bath and County Graphic (Jan. Feb. 1901)

CHAPTER ONE

The Arrival

MRS WORRALL'S DIARY
APRIL 3RD 1817

Today has been most unsuitable, not only has the wind taken down part of the kitchen garden wall, in its falling an old and favourite apple tree has been uprooted and is now to be used as fuel next winter.

A young woman, most weary, has been helped to the hostelry by Mr Overton, our Poorhouse Overseer. At one point the woman (who appears something above twenty years) almost collapsed and had to rely upon Mr Overton's arm for support. I shall call upon her tomorrow as she appears to speak no English and neither Mr Worrall nor Mr Overton could ascertain her place of origin, though they tried to converse with her in all the languages they knew. Mr Overton offered her sixpence, which she REFUSED.

Today my tooth has been aching and I find no solace in peering into my own mouth with the aid of two looking glasses. Something must be done, and my old remedy of hot cloves is of no use. I shall write to Jane (W) to ask her advice.

My Easter Bonnet has arrived and I find it dreadfully DULL. It is not of silk as I thought when I first saw it in Mr Baring's window, but of Barathea, and the ribbons do not please me. It is too late to change it now, and the whole affair has left me with an ill feeling.

Letter from Mrs Worrall of Knole Park
to Jane Worsthorn of Stony Easton Lodge
Good Friday 1817, 2 p.m.

Dearest Jane,

I am LONGING to acquaint you with our latest event at Knole Park. A disturbing arrival here has us all at sixes and sevens and I cannot *think* of a sensible way of concluding such a tangle!

A young woman has walked into Almondsbury in a weary and fatigued condition. She appears unable to speak English or indeed any language known to either Samuel or the Rev. Hunt.

Such consternation as you may well imagine!

With gestures and miming we are all attempting to question and converse with her at once and without any success.

She, the young person I refer to, is well dressed but without money or possessions.

She is of medium height, full figure with an olive skin. She conducts herself in a delicate, sure manner – although she is frequently in tears. Her hands are soft and well kept as if unused to toil of any kind, and she appears to be in great need of help. As we cannot converse, her needs and where she was going remain a mystery.

I thought it best to send her to the public house for the night, sending Stephenson and Bartlett with her to see that no harm came to her. I requested the landlady to prepare a comfortable bed for her in a *private* room, and give her a good supper.

Tomorrow she is to appear before the City Fathers, it being held she is a 'vagrant'. I cannot help but feel an injustice is about to be delivered upon this poor creature, and IMPLORE you to attend this hearing with me that you may also judge her worth and how best I might assist her. I shall acquaint you with all the alarming details of her arrival and behaviour then, though I will indulge here and confess my discomfort at an event which occurred this very morning.

It being Good Friday I rose early and took some necessaries for this person down to the public house where she had lodged for the night. Upon my entering the parlour I discovered her weeping silently. When she saw me, however, she immediately rose and rushed towards me with exclamations of pleasure and threw herself at my feet, bowing her head so low it touched the floor. She then attempted to kiss the hem of my dress – and this in full view of an assembled throng of watchers and idlers! I scarcely knew WHAT to do, but begged her to desist and rise which she did after some few moments.

Mr Hunt then arrived, bringing with him a great supply of books and maps, thinking she might recognise those pictures of her own country. She immediately pointed a finger at CHINA and made us understand she knew this country, but I do not think she is CHINESE for she has not the slant-eyed look.

I did not mention – before I was shewn into the parlour Mrs Pratt, the landlady (a very large and formidable person), drew me aside and told me, in a state of GREAT excitement, how the young woman had refused to sleep in the bed and POINTED TO THE FLOOR as if she did not understand the use of beds! Mrs Pratt quite despaired of making her comfortable, until her little girl Emily climbed into the bed and made the young woman understand what it was for.

THEN the young woman knelt in prayer for what seemed a considerable time, before allowing herself to be persuaded to bed.

Jane, it is FASCINATING!

Mrs Pratt added, she is so well mannered and clean she insists on her cup being WASHED MOST THOROUGHLY after each supply of tea! She also repeats a prayer before and after drinking.

She is SO intelligent. With all the mimicry at my command I managed to convey to her that she should accompany me back to Knole – which she seemed reluctant to do. She did not know where I was taking her, I believe. *Upon our passing the churchyard gate she ran through it and up to the door!* Finding it fastened, she appeared disappointed.

But why should she try to make an escape from me after so warm a greeting?

I believe her to be a CHRISTIAN, for when we arrived at Knole Park, where the servants were at breakfast, she, observing some hot cross buns upon the table, took one. After looking at it earnestly, she cut off the cross and placed it in her dress, in the manner of a crucifix.

Yesterday my same bothersome tooth afflicted me and I am loath to surrender to the awful butcher of a man in Park Street. Can you re-acquaint me with that 'cure' you mentioned? My head being so full I cannot delve deep enough to find past remedies.

Please J. DO COME for I need your clear mind and able assistance. I send this letter to you by 'Peter' who will await your reply.

Affect.
Elizabeth

Letter from Jane Worsthorn of Stony Easton Lodge
to Elizabeth Worrall of Knole Park
Good Friday p.m.

Dear E,

Meet you at Council Chambers.
10 a.m.
REMEDY FOR TOOTHACHE
Morphia, 5 grains.

Affect.
J.W.

CHAPTER TWO

The Workhouse

MRS WORRALL'S DIARY
APRIL 4TH 1817

It being Good Friday we attended 3 services. Mr Worrall read the lesson which came from St Luke Chapter 23, on the Crucifixion.

He reads so well, and I am full of pride as he does so, his voice being so much more melodious than our incumbent, Mr Hunt, who has a somewhat dry tone in this speech. I am sure that everyone notices, for upon leaving the church several persons, inc. Mr and Mrs X. of X., Mrs T. (newly widowed) and the Misses Amelia and Elizabeth Brooking (dry old sticks themselves) were most complimentary.

During the sermon I am afraid to say my own thoughts wandered off into the parable of the Good Samaritan, and being mindful of the 'passers by', thought I may be one myself.

I refer to our *New Arrival*, whose name I have now discovered. My method of discovery was almost by accident and I am still a little self-congratulatory of the occasion . . . It happened thus. After returning from the 11 o-clock service, I withdrew into my 'writing room' and summoned Mrs Pike, requesting she bring our N.A. to me there.

I must now confess to a subterfuge. My inclination being generally rather to talk and let matters unfold in a natural way, I have occasionally noticed, after a meeting, that I have not said all I wished to say upon a subject, as other matters intrude into the occasion. Also I had experienced a wakeful night in trying to fathom how our N.A. had arrived upon these shores, being unable to converse with any person. Doubts entered my mind of this person's honesty . . . consequently I had risen early, and (with many corrections), had written out an address to her which I intended to keep upon my desk as a constant reminder, should my natural *inclination* assert itself.

Mrs Pike returned with our N.A. and considering it best we be alone (for reasons apparent in the address) I asked Mrs Pike to attend to her duties, which she did with much reluctance.

I now append the text of my address:

> 'My good young woman, I very much fear you are imposing on me, and that you can understand and answer me in my own language. If so, and distress has driven you to this expedient, make a friend of me; I am a female as yourself, and can feel for you, and will give you money and clothes and will put you on your journey without disclosing your conduct to any one; but it must be on condition you speak the truth. If you deceive me, I think it is right to inform you that Mr Worrall is a Magistrate and has the power to send you to prison, committing you to hard labour and passing you as a vagrant to your own Parish.'

I was most apprehensive of delivering such a stern address and felt it not a little unworthy, being sensible of the day upon which I had chosen to do so.

During the whole of this address she, (our N.A.), shook her head in an uncomprehending way and immediately began to speak to me in her unknown tongue. Consequently I am in ignorance of what was said. Her appearance was of distress and anger at herself in not being able to converse with me. I am convinced she did not understand my carefully prepared text and for this I feel both relieved and a new anxiety for her plight.

I then received my moment of true inspiration over which I am so pleased. Having made my fearsome speech and waited for her outburst to subside, I took up my pen and wrote my own name upon paper pronouncing it several times and pointing to myself with the pen. Then placing the pen in her hand, I pointed to her, intimating that she must now write her own name down and pronounce it aloud to me.

The pen she declined and I must conclude she cannot write for she shook her head, but after moments of hesitation cried aloud 'C-A-R-A-B-O-O . . . Caraboo . . ,' pointing to herself all the while.

Caraboo is such a strange and beautiful sounding name I am sure I have stumbled upon something and someone extraordinary.

In spite of my protestations to the contrary, she is to be charged tomorrow with 'vagrancy' and I am at a loss to think what shall become of her. Mr Worrall says that it has all gone too far now for him to halt the proceedings as the wretched Mr Overton has already reported her arrival in Almondsbury and such is the law that the wheels of justice once turned must go on turning. Jane (W) is to attend with me and we shall be allowed into the proceedings just so long as we remain silent (says Mr Worrall). He will sit next to his Worship the Mayor and the proceedings are to start at 10 o-clock.

My toothache has subsided but I have the fear it may re-occur at another occasion. I shall hold J.W.'s remedy in reserve.

Committal to Workhouse
St Peter's Hospital for Paupers, Bristol

Date	5th April 1817
Name	Unknown
Sex	Female
Religion	Unknown
Age	Unknown (abt 25 years)
Place of birth	Unknown
Charged with	Vagrancy
Found	Guilty
Sentence	To be placed in St Peter's Hospital until such time as something transpires about her.

CHAPTER THREE

Interest is Aroused

Letter from Jane Worsthorn of Stony Easton Lodge
to Elizabeth Worrall of Knole Park
6th April 1817, p.m.

Dearest E.

I am at a loss to know what to say to you. You have asked for my support and you have also asked for my opinion.

Firstly, the young woman herself. That she is *unlike* any I have ever seen or heard, I do affirm, and in that respect you have my support. Her manner is peculiar, almost as if she has the expectation of being obeyed, which does presume her to be a person of rank in her own country. She neither moves nor walks in such a way I can say is known to me. Her posture is most erect, her back being so very straight that I find it distinctive and not a little puzzling. Her eyes are intelligent and her habit of prolonging her gaze could be alarming if one were not aware of her plight . . . I do not wonder the pig woman ran for assistance when she entered the cottage, so would I have done.

As she is now committed to the Workhouse, I suggest you leave her there for a short period to allow others to assess her story from closer observation.

One of my best greys is down with thrush and cannot travel. I beg you to ask Will Frogley to have a look at him when he can.

J.W.

Letter from Mrs Worrall of Knole Park
to Jane Worsthorn of Stony Easton Lodge
7th April 1817, a.m.

Jane,

You say one of your greys has thrush, but you do not say WHICH. In your stables there are no less than 5 horses, of which three are 'greys'. I think you may be referring to either Clinker or Clasher, whom you have chosen to name after Squire O's famous racehorse and which I warned you about at the time. Now I have spoken to Will Frogley whom I could hardly stop from mounting and riding over to Stony Easton with his whole bag of 'physics'. Should you be able to understand his speech and his endless M'ladys and Marms, you will find him able, for I think him the best groom and judge of horseflesh in the county. He is to ride over tomorrow and will arrive before midday.

We are to have a musical evening, Mr Worrall is agreed, and three musicians are to come from Bristol next Wednesday.

You must sing for us as you know how much we admire and love to hear you – supposing you sing a Schubert Lieder . . . or if you think to prefer something else we shall await your choice with eager anticipation.

Affect.

E.

MRS WORRALL'S DIARY
APRIL 8TH 1817

We are to have a musical evening. Mr Worrall is agreed and I am to arrange the pieces and their order of playing.

The evening, which is to be Thursday 17th April, is to be arranged in three parts and the musicians are to come from Bath and Bristol. I am therefore to send two carriages but not the coach. Mr Worrall has a particularly low opinion of players and says we should send the great cart for all of them in one round trip. J. (W.) is to sing for she has a sweet voice and received lessons as part of her education. Mr Worrall I shall not ASK to sing for although I admire his SPEAKING voice, his SINGING voice is not quite so melodious.

I have received many letters from the Bank today, forwarded from St Peter's by Mrs Treadwell, the matron, who is I fear showing signs of enjoying all this fuss and attention. ALL the letters concern Caraboo, and the news sheets are constantly referring to her. Some of the letters show true concern and all offer some manner of help. Mrs T. has enclosed a note from herself in which she expressed alarm at the number of callers to St P. and is of the opinion that 'C.' is not imposturing as she had been woken many times suddenly in the night by an inmate shaking her, or kicking her – I do trust, gently – and never once did utter or say words of any known language. I shall visit her tomorrow.

MRS WORRALL'S DIARY
APRIL 10TH 1817

Jane has said she cannot or will not sing on the 17th and I shall have to ask one of the girls from Cleve instead. They are unfortunately large, but will make good wives for somebody and the younger, whose name I cannot remember, sings well.

Jane is quite plump now, very pretty face, a few lines, says openly she only married H. for his title. He makes me uncomfortable with his mad eyes and odd manner of speech. Mr Worrall I discover is most fond of Jane, which pleases me as he always says his friends are not my friends, nor my friends, his.

Mr Worrall has sadly remarked my dress to be out of fashion, he means DULL. I do not like this present mode of everything pink, it does not become my colouring and I find this crazed notion we should wear red, white and blue to celebrate the victory tedious. That victory was more than 18 months ago and such a parade of colour worthy of harlots. Autumnal colours of browns and soft russets are best for me and I abhor the use of feathers.

Removed C. from St Peter's yesterday. She had not eaten for three days and drunk only water. Mrs T. most remiss not to have sent word immediately such a situation became known.

As she slept only on the floor she is, in consequence, extremely dirty. She looks so forlorn! Have placed her in rooms above the Bank, which looked lovely when we arrived. C. is so pale after only three days of St P's I do not wonder they all wither there. She greeted me with her customary salaam, kneeling before me in a most decorous manner, but when attempting to rise swayed so dangerously that I feared she might faint. Two persons approached us during the carriage ride – one of the persons said 'she is pretty' and knew her NAME. This was when we were getting into the coach at St Peter's. The ride revived her spirits and she looked so longingly at the tall ships loading in the dock I thought I would cry again. Have surmised I must try to tempt her with rice dishes, that being of the East may appeal to her appetite.

I have located the position of the East Indies on the Globe, it looks very far away – I am firmly resolved to find her people and allow her passage home; most INTERESTING letter came today from a gentleman in Leith who arrived at St Peter's to see her. He suggests her name is not Caraboo but her place of origin is Karabough on the Caspian sea – have also located the Caspian Sea upon the Globe. I shall keep this letter appended to my diary. It will be of great interest in the future.

Leith, April 1817

Madam,

The peculiar case of the unknown female foreigner must naturally excite in the breast of every feeling creature emotions of interest and sympathy. These emotions I perhaps feel in a double degree, from having seen her when in distress. I never can forget the circumstances of my interview with her, nor the gratitude she so eloquently expressed on recognising you, Madam, in the Hospital at Bristol.

Possibly, Madam, you may have no recollection of me, and were it not that I have been an eye-witness of your goodness, I should hesitate much to use the liberty which I now do in addressing you on this subject. You must, however, be so kind as to pardon me for my intrusion, and believe that I should not have troubled you, had I not felt extremely interested in the fate of your protegee.

I think her name is not CARABOO, as stated, but rather that it is her COUNTRY. I consider that she comes from the Bay of Karabough, on the eastern coast of the Caspian sea, and situated in Independent Tartary. She may easily have come from thence by the Persian Gulf, or still more likely by the Black Sea. The latter I consider by far more the likely, as many vessels (many hundreds) have come from the Black Sea to the European ports in the Mediterranean, since the commencement of the present year. I leave these observations, Madam, to your consideration. She might be able to recognize the place I have mentioned on a map, or she might know the names of those places in the immediate vicinity. But you are better able than I am to decide on the manner that this ought to be gone about. I therefore beg to remit it to yourself, and trust that some good may arise from the hint I have taken the liberty of giving you.

I request again, Madam, that you will pardon my presumption in addressing you; and if you will have the goodness to do so, might I still further presume to beg of you to let me know, by some means or other, any thing that you might think proper respecting this interesting fair one.

I am, with the greatest respect,
Madam,
Your most obedient humble Servant
J.S.

CHAPTER FOUR

An Unknown Language

Letter from Mrs Worrall of Knole Park
to Jane Worsthorn of Stony Easton Lodge
April 11th 1817, 4 p.m.

Jane – Come at ONCE! Ride, if you cannot wait for the carriage. (Clasher is, I trust, recovered.) Will Frogley tells me he treated him with his usual potions. Recovery should be swift – don't let the horse do otherwise! I cannot WAIT to tell you my news!

I have brought her back to Knole. (Mr Worrall's rooms above the Bank have been so crammed with visitors I was unable to communicate with C. It was like Market Day there – Mrs Pike quite stiff from so much curtsying – M'Lords and M'ladys flow from her lips as tho' she used such titles daily at Knole!)

Today the Marquis of X. arrived. With him he brought a gentleman from Portugal, a Mr Manuel Eynesso, of whom I had never heard. The Marquis said he hoped Mr Eynesso would understand C.'s language.

Mr Eynesso behaved in the most *gentlemanly* way. (I am told he is from a most distinguished family.) He complimented me on my appearance. (I was wearing my old blue pelisse with the swansdown trimming which is becoming dowdy and quite out of fashion.) He vowed he had taken me for Mr Worrall's daughter!

C. *perfectly* behaved. So gracious as to appear almost condescending. It was as though she was of higher rank than either of the men.

BUT – and here is the interest of my story – Mr Eynesso listened MOST attentively while C. spoke, then begged permission to converse with her. Needless to say I complied.

After several minutes – I need hardly tell you, Jane, I was BREATHLESS with expectation – he announced he understood her language! Her face had

19

become so animated, I knew instantly this was so, and a lump came to my throat to see her so happy.

Mr Eynesso told us her language is a dialect from Islands in the East, and not a pure language, which is why she is so difficult to understand. He mentioned Sumatra. He hinted at her being a Princess, and told us she was abducted from her island home and brought to England – for what nefarious purpose she could not tell him. But we can guess.

I was right, Jane, to see in her a person of good breeding. I could tell at once from the way she behaved that she was no imposter but someone of importance. I beg you to come and help me. Between us we can surely make sense of what she says. Mr Eynesso left for London immediately after the interview; he is due back in Portugal in a few days. He visited Bristol only by chance, to sup with his old friend the Marquis of X.

C. has just entered the room. She is looking at this letter as I write, and smiling at me, for writing fascinates her. It must be the pen and ink, and the squiggles we make with them! It is SO sad she cannot understand what I am saying, but she *must* comprehend the warmth of her welcome here!

She salaamed and kissed the hem of my dress just now. When I begged her to desist she endeavoured to repeat the performance, thinking I was encouraging her. I must try to emphasise that these manners are not 'de rigeur' in England!

Affect.
Elizabeth

MRS WORRALL'S DIARY
APRIL 13TH 1817

Jane's coming here has been such a comfort. The first evening I was not so sure. Jane told me there was no 'proof' C. was not an imposter. Must not become too 'carried away'. Mr Worrall returned from the Bank, full of gloom. Would not talk to me. Muttered something about 'ruin'. I asked him if he was ill. He said 'no' but looked quite pale. I cannot make him understand I am interested in his business affairs. The war is making some bother at the Bank, I believe.

He became cheerful when Jane arrived, and insisted that she sing to him after supper. I fear J. is something of a flirt. I had never noticed what large hands she has. At the piano they looked quite masculine. And her voice is not as true as it was. Mr Worrall leant over the piano and turned the pages for her most attentively. She discarded her shawl saying she felt 'too warm'.

Too warm indeed! The room was like an ice house. I was huddled in my pilgrim's cloak AND I was near the fire. Her shoulders, I have heard say, are her best feature. Puce does not become her. The colour makes her skin look sallow. C. listened to the music with rapt attention.

When the singing finished, C. looked upwards, as though to say 'what a heavenly thing, such music is!' She clapped her hands together, like a child. We entreated HER to perform, but she shook her head, though understanding from our gestures what we wanted. At length she seemed persuaded and intimated that she would like my glass bowl, which was full of oranges. I assented, somewhat nervously, I confess. It is a rare object, Murano glass, and very fragile. I did not know what she would do with it.

She held it in one hand, assuming an infinite variety of attitudes, bending her body in numberless shapes. Placing the bowl on the floor, she danced around it, first dropping on one knee, then rising with uncommon agility and holding up one foot in a sling. She performed a species of waltz with the most singular twists and turns. We could not tear our eyes away from her. She contorted her body so gracefully that she never risked giving the slightest offence.

At length she picked up the bowl and presented it to me, balancing it on the tips of her fingers and thumb, with the utmost grace and delicacy.

She is like some enchanting *wild* animal. A panther, perhaps, though I have never seen one. Mr Worrall is charmed, and even J. admitted she had never seen dancing of THAT quality before.

I believe Jane is becoming enchanted with C. though she still warns me not to be 'foolish'. She has been sitting with C. and I for over two hours, books before us on the table and the candles lit. A map is spread out upon the floor. We are attempting to re-trace C.'s journey across the oceans.

Tomorrow J. leaves. Mr Worsthorn is anxious lest she has decided to become a fixture at Knole.

MRS WORRALL'S DIARY
APRIL 22ND 1817

A dear and revered old friend, the Rev. Tucker, now more than 70 years of age, came to visit me at Knole today. I do fear he still treats me in exactly the same way as he did when I was six years old. His hair is now quite white and sparse, though he still wears his own. Wigs, he always said, were man's abomination, and to prove his point he has grown whiskers (also quite white). The whole effect is that of an amiable sheep. His eyes are still the same remarkable light blue I remember and I do retain a suspicion in my mind that were I alone he would not have made the journey. Caraboo's fame and reputation is responsible for that.

He called a little after three p.m. having journeyed over from Bath where he now lives in retirement. He is in good health, though a little frail and his journey was 'bumpty' he said. 'Bumpty' is such a word. He complained that the roads were so bad they near shook the teeth out of his head, and he was cramped and hot when he arrived.

He had come in a dog cart of rather heavy make, so old as to be unsprung, and drawn by a lovely gay old chestnut named 'Solomon' who was, I fear, showing signs of age also. I recommended some of Birch's Oil Rub and two days' rest upon his return – though I suspect that my piece of advice will go unheeded. I should dearly love to see the saddle, for I fear it may be showing signs of age too. I think my old friend's stable to be of the one horse variety. Solomon will of necessity treble as hack, hunter and carriage animal. I left Will Frogley frowning and clicking his teeth at such misuse of one of God's creatures as he led the way to his famous 'physic' stall. Solomon was in better condition when he left for the return journey.

The afternoon was not uneventful but I fear not a great success. We had sat to tea. Caraboo, upon being introduced to our guest, made the deepest obeisance, almost touching the floor with her forehead, then salaamed as to a male person of rank – that is she inclines her head to the right side (to the left side for a woman). She then raises her right hand palm outwards to lightly touch her forehead with the back of her hand. It is all very pretty and her smile is so charming and disarming I was unprepared for what happened next.

My old and trusted friend the Rev. Tucker behaved in the oddest way. 'You are', he said, staring at Caraboo intently, 'the most beautiful creature I have ever seen.' Caraboo remained motionless. No blush appeared on her cheek and it was as if she had not heard. Her expression was one of calm indifference and remained so – clearly she had not understood what was said. The Rev. Tucker then moved his chair a little closer to her, still staring at her all the while. 'You are an angel,' he persisted. I am pleased to say C. did not appear disturbed by this untoward behaviour although I *did* notice the beginnings of a frown. It was only then that I recovered enough to stop such monstrous conduct.

I said 'Sir, this is too forward of you', or something similar. 'If you are hoping to surprise Caraboo and cause her distress by this flattery, speak no more, for you are wasting your breath. I *know* she cannot understand our language. She knows several words which I myself have taught her, but that is all. You presume upon my goodwill sir by this quizzing, and I bid you to refrain from it.'

CHAPTER FIVE

Life at Knole

Today C. surprised us all by diving into the lake FULLY CLOTHED! We had been walking in the Spring sunshine admiring the new plantation of flowering trees, when C. ran up the bank, threw up her hands, and dived into the water! Mr Worrall and I had been accompanied in our walk by the Misses Brooking (they were unable to keep away a moment longer – their curiosity, like their noses, is sharp). They wished to 'interview' C.

Can you imagine our horror? Not only did C. disappear from view for several moments (Mr Worrall chivalrously preparing to divest himself of jacket and boots and dive in after her) – but when she reappeared she swam with great strength to the island. Her swimming, Mr Worrall says, resembles the 'dog' paddle, taught to children. On reaching the island she waved to us, then disappeared among the trees. Here she stayed some time. Miss Amelia Brooking was quite beside herself, walking up and down the bank, pointing with her parasol and shouting 'Come back! Come back at once!' I fear I told her she was making a great deal of fuss and C. did not understand what she was saying. I thought for one moment she would join C. in the lake, but Mr Worrall caught her by the arm. Miss Elizabeth was, I think, the more offended of the two, for she had been telling C. of the pains in her stomach before being left in such a peremptory way. C. of course, mercifully, did not comprehend a word. Miss Elizabeth became quite rude about C., calling her a 'savage'. She mentioned she feared I would be 'contaminated' by contact with C. I fear she is jealous. So much attention is being paid to C. and so many important visitors are arriving at Knole.

When C. emerged from the water her dress clung to her body as though she wore no clothes. Mr Worrall I noticed, looked at her with interest. C.

ran back to the house, attempting to hide from the prying eyes of the gardeners by dodging between the trees.

'How shocking,' Miss Amelia Brooking said to me, 'You will no doubt stop *that savage* behaving in such a way in future.'

I could scarcely believe my ears.

Mr Worrall pointed out many people found bathing health-giving and cleansing. He added C. was fully clothed and perfectly 'decent'.

Soon after, the Misses Brooking left.

I have rarely seen visitors leave in such a hurry. They will, no doubt spread gossip through the neighbourhood.

Afterwards Mr Worrall said to me, 'She has a fine figure'. I knew to whom he was referring.

I do so dislike the way men react to the Female Body. It is most provoking when one is no longer Young.

MRS WORRALL'S DIARY
KNOLE PARK. APRIL 28TH

Today, a most bothersome episode occurred. C. has made herself a temple to Allah Tallah on the island in the lake. Here she worships twice a day, walking three times round the temple, sprinkling water over it before she kneels to pray, covering her head with a shawl before she kneels. I have decided to note down each thing she does (for future reference, for it may help us discover her identity). It is a charming ceremony. Mr Worrall rows me across the lake to watch. The temple itself is about two foot high, being a cross hatch of twigs, something in the manner of a Wig Wam. C. has wreathed it in flowers and leaves, mainly wild flowers and laurel leaves. I do not know if this is significant. Here she often comes to prepare and eat her food.

Peterson – Mr Worrall's valet – such a swarthy, greasy young man – I do not trust him – came running to me today to inform me C. can understand and speak English! He was rowing her across the lake (though she likes to row herself, she will accept help if she is burdened, and she was carrying three pigeons to 'sacrifice' to Allah Tallah and then eat herself). He tells me he waited until they were in the middle of the lake – for there she could not pretend so easily – and then told her 'Caraboo is a cheat. Caraboo talks English as well as I do!' (I can imagine his nasty, jeering tone as he said this. He has ALWAYS doubted her. Such an unpleasant man!) Caraboo was naturally startled. Peterson tells me she replied immediately 'Caraboo no cheat.' He says her accent is perfect, and she appeared to understand his accusation with no trouble.

When he laughed and cried 'you see, you DO understand English, you are not a foreigner at all!' (HORRID HORRID man), C. rose to her feet and rocked the boat as tho' intending to tip him in the water.

Now I KNOW C. is intelligent. This has been proved time and time again. She is learning English fast. I am SURE she has picked up the word 'cheat' from someone. After all, so many people have accused her of it! I am certain that she was able to understand the meaning of his words well enough to mimic them in reply.

I confess to a niggling doubt, however, and mentioned my fears to Mrs Pike. She confirms that C. has never, never uttered any English words. Her language has always been consistent.

I am noting down words and their meanings every day – it will be interesting to present a new language to the scholars! I intend to send a copy to Oxford University. C. *never* pronounces a word or a syllable of language resembling English. We test her all the time. Mrs Pike sleeps with her, and listens to hear if she talks in her sleep, and sometimes she DOES talk, but always in her own language. Returning in the carriage with me from Bristol, she is sometimes so fatigued she falls asleep – I have, I confess, woken her suddenly to surprise her – but not a word or a sound not in her own 'lingo', as we call it, escapes her.

I cannot, I just CANNOT, believe C. is an imposter.

MRS WORRALL'S DIARY
KNOLE PARK. APRIL 27TH

Today my notes will concern C.'s food and her manner of eating it. Her diet consists mainly of rice, which she prefers to bread. She drinks only water and tea. All her food she prepares herself (and makes it very savoury). She is fond of Indian curry. She ALWAYS prays to Allah Tallah before allowing any food or drink to pass her lips.

To perform her 'sacrifice' to Allah Tallah (if such it is) she takes a pigeon, rabbit or fish and beheads it, burying the head in the earth, together with the blood. She then kneels in prayer to Allah Tallah, facing the spot where the head is buried. For this, she covers her head in her shawl. When she has done praying (and it usually lasts some minutes) she collects wood and makes a fire. The headless carcase is wrapped in mud, and, when the fire is burning well, placed in the hottest part to roast. I have tried the meat, and found it delicious. C. sometimes holds little parties round the fire, and several of us gather to worship and dine with her. Mr Worrall says the gypsies cook in a similar way. C. NEVER omits grace before the meal. We are made to look quite heathen against her devotion!

After dining she washes her face and hands in the lake. She brushes her hair by her reflection in the water also, and this is a delight to watch.

On Tuesdays she fasts on the roof of the Tower; a most dangerous and difficult climb which she attempts at peril of her life. I cannot stop her. I offered her Mr Worrall's small Turkish prayer rug from the library to kneel on, but she refused, making signs that it might be damaged by the weather. I have begged her not to climb on the roof, but it seems to be the most important part of her religion and she will not be dissuaded.

EVERYTHING she does reinforces my belief that she is what I feel her to be. I am FORCED to the conclusion C. is genuine. So much of what she does is what I would expect from the native of some half-civilised island.

Letter from Elizabeth Worrall of Knole Park
to Jane Worsthorn of Stony Easton Lodge
April 29th 1817, a.m.

Dearest Jane,

You asked me to let you know how C. is faring – I cannot THINK why you do not ride over to see for yourself. You SAY you are busy, but busy on WHAT? If it is your dressmaker, then it is time you came here to show me the latest models! I fear I am sadly out of fashion. I hear there is a new bonnet named the Wellington (or is it OATLANDS?) It is to do with the war in any case.

My dear, a positive CAVALCADE of carriages comes up the drive each day. The village is all agog and lines the street to watch. Coaches, broughams, phaetons, gigs, even charyots – and, of course, our visitors also ride over. It is a veritable fashion show!

Most of the visitors bring C. gifts. I have stationed Wilkes at the door, with orders to accept the gift and unwrap it, placing it upon a table in the hall so that C. can admire it at her leisure. Each article is brought in the hope that it is from C.'s country, but so far no one has yet found an article that comes from her island. We have been given SUCH oddities! Brass dishes with scratches on them which are thought to be a language, watercolour paintings of ships, volcanoes and islands, portraits of strange savage chieftains, ugly black wooden masks, knobbed canes, trumpets, bits of materials and shells, large stones of volcanic rock, jewellery (some of it is quite interesting – I tried on a necklace of beaten copper and C. was

26

delighted with it). So much of what we are given is of no use whatever, and we cannot even ascertain what they are FOR!

C. is enchanted with all the fuss. She runs backward and forward between the visitors and the gifts, and as each gift is opened she gives little OOOHS and AAAAHS of pleasure and holds it in her hands to examine it properly. If she feels inclined, she will dance for the assembled visitors.

Wilkes must have new livery. The old one is spotted and rubbed with age. Jane, is your dressmaker fashionable? Mine is, I fear, failing. Her eyesight is not as careful as it was, and her eye for colour is not mine. Also the Paris dolls have not arrived. This wretched war! We are becoming Country Bumpkins. I have ordered a pelisse gown as a half dress. It is of red Italian silk, trimmed with squirrel. I shall wear it over white muslin, as is the fashion. I have not heard if Clasher is recovered? Will Frogley has been busy medicating Belmont, who has bad teeth, and is finding it difficult to eat.

My tooth is also bothersome. C. bathes my forehead with eau de cologne when I am in agony. She has such a soothing, gentle touch. Mr Worrall says it is a rotted black tooth. He peered into my mouth and said 'that tooth must go.' But Jane, who will pull it? I am sure it will be more painful to have it drawn than to keep it in.

Do come. We await your visit with great eagerness. I am netting myself an overdress of yellow cotton. My netting box is a constant source of amusement for C., with the wooden netting needles and gauges. She is interested by the flat fork shape and the netting clamp. Today she made off with one of my netting needles, having stuck it in her hair to beautify herself! I had to laugh, but insisted she gave it back. She is always trying the lotions on my dressing table. White powder makes her sneeze, but she pats it on her face in imitation of me, then grimaces, as if to say 'this does not suit me'. She is *such* a delight to be with. I am feeling young again. Even Mr Worrall approves. I found them fencing together in the garden. Mr Worrall had found his old fencing foils and was teaching C. how to use them. After several bouts she managed to disarm him and he was not pleased and said to me 'the sun was in his eyes!'

I was NOT pleased to see Peterson, Stephens, Wilkes, Mrs Pike, Will Frogley and Martha gathered at the windows to see the affair, also the gardeners, who hovered in the distance pretending to cut the hedges. They hoped I could not see them. I was even more astonished when Mrs Pike appeared beside me, on the pretext she had a message to give me. The message was, she had run out of silk to mend Mr Worrall's stockings!.

Affect.

E.

Captain Palmer called this morning. He has been in Edinburgh, visiting an Aunt, and he was amazed to find C.'s fame had spread so far north! He is a good neighbour (though choleric when it is wet, for then his wooden leg plagues him).

He came to visit just when I collapsed, exhausted, on the sofa, after an endless stream of visitors. C. had found my smelling salts, and was applying them to my nose.

Brusque as usual, Capt. Palmer told C. not to salaam to him, for it made him uncomfortable. She looked quite hurt. I said 'Capt. Palmer, she is only following the custom of her country. She salaams to everyone.' 'Not to me, Ma'am, she don't,' he replied. He is a man known for his plain speaking. He brought with him a great array of maps and books. He and C. and I sat round the library table while he opened them to show us pages of interest.

He is a most FASCINATING man, and such a traveller! My knowledge of geography, hitherto slight, is becoming extensive. We have discovered the name of the Captain of the Pirate Ship (Chee Min). He is copper coloured, wears a turban, short petticoat trowsers and a kind of scarf thrown over his shoulders. Capt. Palmer has ascertained the Pirate Prow has only one mast and no gun, and her colours are the Venetian war colours. The sails of Chee Min's boat are seamed up and down, and a different shape from Javasu boats, whose sails are of matting or rush. The Chinese sails are made ACROSS, with split bamboo sticks. C. made out she could not tell what colours were hoisted at different ports. She closed her eyes, and placed her fingers on her eyelids, shaking her head to show she was blindfold and kept below in the ship throughout the journey. My heart aches with the thought of the misery she must have undergone!

My toothache returned again this evening. Merely a Twinge, but a foretaste of things to come. I MUST have it Pulled. Most dentists are but Quacks with Forceps. I do fear the pain of it.

CHAPTER SIX

In which the Manner of Caraboo's Appearance in England is Discovered

Letter from Mrs Worrall of Knole Park
to Jane Worsthorn of Stony Easton Lodge
May 2nd 1817

Dear J.,

You have not come, though I begged you to. C.'s story is taking shape, and we are now able to form a clearer picture. Capt. Palmer has been most conscientious. When there is a lull between visitors he takes C. to the library, and there they sit, he with his pen and his papers, writing down all he discovers.

C. is now dressed in the manner of her country. Without letting her know, I took the carriage to Bristol, and how grateful I was I had not invited her. Belmont bolted (my dear, I have rarely been so frightened!) Some great yapping fool of a dog at his heels. The carriage was near tipping over. Will Frogley had difficulty restraining him from jumping a hedge (as you know, he is a powerful animal and chestnuts are HOT). Will lashed at the dog with his whip, but this made it worse, for it maddened the brute. My carriage hat (a new one, you have not seen it, MADLY patriotic, I succumbed to the fashion at last – white silk trimmed with red and blue ribands) flew off, my muff and tippett fell to the floor, and I clung to the handle for dear life. The animal left us at the crossroads, not a second too soon. He had a nasty look about him, and I feared his return. We spent some time adjusting ourselves when Belmont finally halted. Of course, all Will thought about was his precious horse, whom he examined from hoof to teeth to make sure no injury had occurred. Little thought was spared for ME. Will wondered if Belmont's bad teeth had been instrumental in his flying off in such a fashion.

At Mr Dancy's we must have spent quite half an hour in discussion. C.'s complexion, height, weight, the climate of Javasu and the suitability of different materials were all touched on. At his persuasion I bought a length of cream coloured calico which I think is suitable for her, being neither too loud in colour nor too flimsy. Gauzes are all the rage, Mr Dancy tells me. Ladies damp them to their bodies to show off their figures. I do not think I will indulge in such frolics at my age. Will you, Jane ?

On my return I presented the cloth to C. She was SO pleased! The cloth fascinated her. She held it to the light, rubbed it against her cheek, fingering it in the most delicate way. I felt touched she should be SO grateful. There is so LITTLE we can do for her.

I explained that I wished her to make herself a dress in the style to which she was accustomed in Javasu. Capt. Palmer has discovered that when she was captured in Javasu she was wearing a gown worked in gold, with a shawl embroidered in gold around her head. Her clothes were so soaked with sea water, and so torn, that she wished to change them. She knocked on the door of a cottage (the door was painted green) and was given the clothes she wore when she arrived in Almondsbury – a black stuff gown, cotton shawl, leather sandals and various other articles, in which dress, after wandering around for six weeks, she arrived here, to me. She lived off charity all this while. Capt. Palmer thinks it will be impossible to trace the cottage where she changed her clothes, for the description is of no use.

Jane, the new dress is *charming*. She completed it in two days. I was curious, so peeped around the door, to discover Mrs Pike and C. sewing as if their lives depended on it. I believe Mrs Pike has become so fond of C. that she herself did most of the sewing. They sewed until it was quite dark, C. appearing only to collect candles or receive visitors. I warned her it was not good for her eyes. C. has a strange habit of clicking her teeth and making guttural sounds when she is pleased. When she came to show me the dress, I could tell she was delighted.

It is short, to the knee, displaying her fine calves and ankles. I had not noticed until now that she had quite large feet. They are surprising in one of noble blood, carried always on the shoulders of men. In Javasu I believe they go barefoot round the house (which is broadening to the feet). C. has embroidered (in Mrs Pike's tapestry wools) a band of green and gold around the bosom of the dress, the sleeves and the hem. The sleeves are long and odd-shaped, scored up at the elbow, in fashion Chinese. The dress is simple but striking. C. has the appearance of an Amazon huntress and needs only bows and arrows and feathers in her hair. Come soon! I am longing to show her to you!

Affect.

E.

*Letter from Jane Worsthorn of Stony Easton Lodge
to Mrs Worrall of Knole Park
May 2nd 1817, 4 p.m.*

Dear Elizabeth,

My grey mare, Duchess, is in foal. Clasher still suffers from thrush, and I myself have a cold in the head. I do not feel like venturing abroad just yet. I fear I caught my ailment from that dash across the country side in pouring rain, to welcome Caraboo.

I admit she is interesting.

I am lying here with hot chocolate on a tray and Françoise in attendance. She has orders that no one may disturb me.

Send more news of C. Your letters read like Romances. I am avid for details. Why *not* buy feathers for her hair?

Affect.
J.W.

*Letter from Mrs Worrall of Knole Park
to Jane Worsthorn of Stony Easton Lodge
May 3rd 1817*

Dearest Jane,

How very sorry I am that you are ill! Stay in bed, keep warm, and you will be well in no time. Keep all the windows closed, and heap as many bedclothes upon you as you can stand the weight, and the fire burning.

So provoking! Bertha, the dairymaid, is with child by a gypsy. I am at a loss to know WHAT to do. She is good in the dairy, but a big bosom and blue eyes, and the men have been paying too much attention to her. Shall I send her away, or keep her and the child? It is of great importance to do *right*, for I do not wish to make the girl virtuous by seeming to condone her misfortune!

You ask for more news of C. Since you sound so interested, I am enclosing Capt. Palmer's notes. He has been most thorough. I have learned so much in the last few days! He is away today, for the wet weather has given him twinges in the leg and he fears to lose his temper with C. He has the patience of an angel! Often, when she does not understand what he says, he will repeat the question in various forms, continuing until she at last grasps his meaning.

We are occupied learning words and whole sentences from her. I tell her people will be astounded by our fluency in her tongue, should we visit Javasu. I have learnt how to say 'sleep well','good morning' and the like; 'please' does not seem to be in C.'s vocabulary. In Javasu they say 'it is well', or 'I want'. Never 'thank you'.

C. calls her father's country 'Congee' which Capt. Palmer thinks must be China. Her mother is from the 'Maudins' meaning the Malays. The island they inhabit is, as you know, Javasu. Forgive me if I have told you these details already. I am so forgetful I am sure I repeat myself!

C. described her mother's teeth as being blackened. (Capt. Palmer thinks this must be the Betel Nut, chewed in many places in the East.) Her face and arms are painted, and she wears a jewel in her nose, with a gold chain from it, fastened at the left temple with a jewelled pin. Capt. Palmer asked why C. did not wear such an ornament herself? When she understood him, she made out that her father wished her to be more European. Her father has three other wives, and is carried on the shoulders of the Macratoos (common men) in a kind of sedan chair or palanquin.

I enclose some notes of Capt. Palmer's which you may like to have.

I allow C. the complete freedom of the house and garden and encourage her to point out things of interest to her. In this way Capt. Palmer and I have been able to glean much valuable information. She remarks upon every object in the house, holding it, shaking it, sniffing it, and on some occasions putting it in her mouth. I warned her that this could be dangerous, if the object were poisonous. To accompany her gestures she makes various sounds, suggestive of anything from admiration to disgust. Her curiosity is insatiable.

She has picked up, at various times, a Chinese chain purse, a rose coloured scarf (which she put on, first in the Chinese fashion, and afterwards, in the Javasu fashion, in both instances veiling her face), a pierced ivory fan, a Chinese puzzle, Indian ink, white and brown sugar candy, and green tea, saying 'Congee'. This, as you remember, is her father's country.

Cinnamon, white pepper, rice, mother of pearl, flying fish, are from Javasu, and coco nuts, long peppers and coral, are from the Malay country.

I am looking at objects in the house with new interest. Each time we find curios forgotten in the attic (Mr Worrall's father, that tiresome old man, was much travelled as you remember), we present them to C. and anxiously watch her reaction. Names such as Sumatra, Congee, Borneo and Javasu are as familiar to me now as Almondsbury, Bath or Bristol.

Mrs Pike has mended Mr Worrall's silk stockings so finely that I cannot complain of her taking time to help C. with her stitching.

Come SOON, Jane. I *have* bought feathers for C.'s hair, as you suggested. We have found her a drum, also a bow and some arrows, in the attic.

Affect.

E.

CAPT. PALMER'S NOTES

Description of Caraboo's father

Wore a gold button in his cap. Three peacock feathers on right side of head, gold chain twisted around neck, from which suspended square locket of amber coloured stone, set in gold. Father's name Jessee Mandu.

Father's position

Had command of soldiers. When any person approached him, they made their salaam or obeisance on both knees, lifting the right hand to the right temple. Presentation of fruit on a dish was with the dish balanced on the points of the fingers, kneeling on both knees to Caraboo's father, but on one knee to Caraboo herself.

During dinner the Macratoos (common men) played to her father upon an instrument consisting of a reed through which they blew. This was fixed to a kind of harp held between the knees and played with the fingers.

Father's complexion was white. He was 47 years old.

Caraboo's name had been Sissu Mandu, which was afterwards changed to Caraboo, in consequence of her father having conquered his enemies.

General Notes

Servants salaam to gentlemen with the right hand, to ladies with the left.

Boogoos (cannibals) are black. When they take white prisoners they cut off their heads and arms, and roast them by a fire, round which they dance, then they eat them.

Worship

When shown the picture of an idol, the object of worship at Prince's island, Caraboo expressed the greatest abhorrence and implied that SHE did not worship such a thing. She worshipped Allah Tallah, and her mother told her if she did as her father did – and prayed to an image – she would be burnt in a fire.

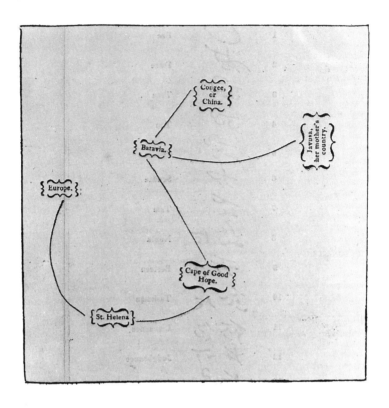

Caraboo's chart showing her voyage to Britain *British Library*

Notes on the voyage

The Pirate Prow belonging to Chee Min had only one mast and no guns. The colours were the Venetian war colours. Chee Min, the commander, was copper coloured, wore a turban, short petticoat trowsers, and a kind of scarf thrown over his shoulders.

Tappa Boo, commander of the second vessel, had a dark complexion, long black whiskers, long black hair plaited down the back, knotted at the end in a bow. He wore a kind of sealskin cap, and an earring in his right ear.

Tappa Boo's brig had 40 men, and Caraboo could not say how many guns. Among the men was a Justee (Surgeon). The vessel carried the Spanish colours.

The purpose of her abduction is not clear. It seems slavery might have been the object.

How it happened was thus

Caraboo was walking in the garden with her three women (sammen). Chee Min and his men surrounded her and carried her off. Caraboo's father, in attempting to rescue her, shot an arrow and killed one of her attendants. She herself wounded two of Chee Min's men with her crease (dagger), one of whom died, but the other one recovered with the help of the Justee.

After 11 days Caraboo was sold to Tappa Boo. Caraboo was conveyed from one ship to the other by boat.

After four weeks the brig anchored at a port (Batavia?) and remained there two days. Four female passengers were taken on board. The ladies would talk and write, but Caraboo could not understand them, nor they her.

Tappa Boo bought Caraboo from Chee Min with a bag of gold dust. After Tappa Boo bought her, she was very ill. The Justee cupped her in the back of the neck and bled her in the arm and wrist. Her hair, which had been long, was cut off. She was confined to her bed for a considerable time.

When asked WHY she was ill, she made out it was through her crying and general unhappiness in consequence of her miserable and forlorn situation.

After being in the brig five weeks more they anchored at another port (the Cape of Good Hope?) where the four females landed. Here they stayed three days and then sailed for Europe, which was reached in 11 weeks.

Being near some part of the coast of England she jumped overboard and swam to shore.

CHAPTER SEVEN

Caraboo goes to Church

*Letter from Jane Worsthorn of Stony Easton Lodge
to Mrs Worrall of Knole Park
May 10th 1817*

Dearest E.

My cold has gone. Clasher is recovered. Curiosity has me by the nose. I shall stay several days. Are you expecting company? Are you pleased?

Mr Worsthorn will not, of course, accompany me. His 'Proof of Life Everlasting' buries him in ink and bad temper. It is a very difficult subject to argue and he has been reduced to Shouting.

Affect.
Jane

MRS WORRALL'S DIARY
MAY 11TH 1817, 8 P.M.

Jabez Carter died last week, and was buried yesterday. I was invited to the Wake, also the servants. Jabez was a crusty old man, but a good carpenter. I could never easily look at him, for the wart on his face was so very large.

Jane decided to accompany me to the Wake. We explained to C. where we intended to go, and begged her to come with us. She refused. She had seen Jabez in his coffin in the lychgate of the church and asked us, what it was. We told her, a dead person. Would this happen to her, she made signs to ask, if she 'bardoo' (died) while at Knole? Though I told her she was a strong, healthy girl, and unlikely to die just yet, I had to confess that this was how she would be buried. She shook her head and stamped her foot. 'I, not die!' she exclaimed. Her English is getting better. She copies our words, in such a way, with such freshness and innocence, that, charming though it is, it is sometimes difficult to understand her meaning – but we generally know what she is TRYING so hard to say. She accompanies her monosyllables with signs and sounds.

C. made out, by gestures, that in her father's country, all corpses are burnt. She, too, wished to be burnt. How thankful I was that Jane was with me! We comforted her as best we could, but she would NOT go to the church for the funeral, nor to Jabez' wake.

When we returned, we found her GONE!

Jane and I called and called. We searched everywhere. We summoned all the servants to help us look for her. Will Frogley suggested setting out on old Belcher, who can scarce trot, to scour the countryside.

Perhaps, I thought, she may be 'teasing' us. Any moment she will appear, and make us laugh!

I confess, I became distraught.

'There must be a simple explanation,' said Jane and as she said these words a cry came from the garden – 'She is found!'

The old gardener, Joseph, heard a noise in the cedar tree, looked up, and found her sitting in the topmost fork! As a gardener he is useless, being too old, but his hearing is acute for birdsong. He is always on the look out for a new arrival in the spring – and the rustling from the cedar made him imagine some large bird had arrived !

We surrounded the tree and pleaded with C. to descend. She was reluctant, but finally agreed. Why should she climb a tree? Why did she not answer when we called? Joseph thinks she was frightened – but of WHAT? Jane said she must have found it easier to climb the tree than to get down again, and was in all probability, stuck.

When she finally came down to earth she was cold and very scratched on her arms and legs. Jane scolded her for being so thoughtless. I took her hands in mine, and begged her not to hide again. Tears filled her eyes at having caused us such anxiety, but she would not tell us why she had climbed the tree.

At length Mrs Pike, with her usual gentle persistence, drew from her the explanation that she had been frightened at finding herself alone in the house, and climbed the tree to escape contamination from men!

Such modesty on her part fills me with apprehension. I cannot always be with her. I did not realise the full extent of her fears in a strange country.

It is SO difficult to care for her properly!

My new jewellery has arrived. It is perhaps a LITTLE bold – but since C. has been here I have become so influenced by her exotic style! The gold earrings are a trifle heavy, and the tasselled silver necklace with jade may be 'un peu vulgaire' – but C. is so admiring of my new acquisitions I am constantly tempted to buy more! I have recently discovered a love of feathers. This is C.'s doing. She gave a cry of pleasure, and clapped her hands, pirouetting upon one foot, when I showed her my new saffron turban with the ostrich plumes. My embroidered mantle likewise took her fancy. The Indian scarf she borrowed from me to drape around her own shoulders, and so showed herself to me. She looked quite charming! I had a mind to give it to her, but Mr Worrall is becoming DREADFULLY mean. Can the Bank REALLY be in such trouble? His long face when I showed him my dressmaker's bill was quite horrid. The milliner's bill is still to come. It almost spoilt my day. I CANNOT entertain in the greys and browns I wore formerly. They are such dowdy colours. I have a fancy for turquoise, and orange, and gold. Lady T. wore a beaver trimmed bonnet when I last saw her, and looked so smart, I vow I wished I had a bonnet of similar style.

We have had such a day.

C. appeared at breakfast in full war panoply, and by monosyllables and gestures gave us to understand it was her father's birthday. Finding a length of string, she knotted it to show us he would be 47 years old. She must have been born when her father was in his twenties. *How* he must miss her!

She had roped a gong (so clever – *such* ingenuity!) to her back. I recognised it as being one we kept in the attic – Mr Worrall will NOT throw away his father's 'treasures' and how thankful I am now that he did not!

The gong sounded in a singular manner, 'BOOM BOOM!' which brought the servants running to see what was happening. Soon they were peering round the doorway – much to my annoyance. I must speak to Wilkes about it. No work is done in house or garden when C. is about.

I asked C. to turn around so that I could admire her. This she did. She was as fully dressed for 'war' as anyone I have ever imagined. On one side she carried her 'sword' – a well-shaped stick. Over her left shoulder was slung a bow and a quiver full of arrows. In her right hand she rattled a tambourine (I cannot think where she found *that*). Her head was dressed with flowers and feathers, and a branch or two of laurel, and her face was painted in stripes, with charcoal.

The gong she was sounding in the most original manner, by arching her back and letting it fall against her buttocks, where it hit a wooden pad belted to the small of her back. The noise was very loud. It quite startled Stumpy, who shot out of the room as fast as her legs could carry her. I have not seen her so active since she bit Mr Hunt.

C. gave me a most warlike grimace, stretching her lips wide over her teeth. 'Me, WAR,' she announced, unnecessarily, smiling happily.

I said we were soon to go to church. 'Me, come,' she answered. 'No,' I told her, 'you are not dressed properly. Take off your war paint and accoutrements, then you may come.' 'Father, birthday,' she replied. She then made a long speech in 'Javasu', the gist of which I think I understood correctly, which was, that it was the custom in Javasu to dress in such a way to honour one's parent's birthday. Anything less would be a lack of respect.

'But the congregation will look at YOU and not listen to Mr Hunt,' I told her. She did not seem to understand. 'You *cannot* come to church like that,' I added. But I COULD NOT dissuade her. I DO like her coming to church, for here she can see Christianity at 'home' so to speak, even if she cannot understand what is happening.

The servants came with us, as always. Mr Worrall was to read the lesson. We started down the hill – the walk to church is pleasant in dry weather, and Mr Worrall and I led the way. After a short while C. came running after us, the gong bumping on her back. 'She is surely not coming like that,' said Mr Worrall, sounding cross. I told him it was C.'s father's birthday. 'That does not excuse her wearing such a . . . a . . . ' he was at a loss for words. Finally he spluttered, 'such a damned cannonade of musical instruments!' C. did not, of course, understand him, but I was afraid the servants would hear. 'You will kindly keep quiet during the service,' he snapped at C.

I could not very well ask C. not to accompany us to church. I had begged her to come so many times. What could I do? Mr Worrall looked quite forbidding. He was wearing his new broad-cloth coat with green facings and gilt buttons. He looked so handsome in it. I was sorry to see him so cross.

Our entrance into church created a sensation. It was a trial for us all. We were a trifle late (Mr Worrall having stopped our procession in an attempt to dissuade C. from joining us) and I had left my reticule in the library. Mr Hunt had waited the service for us. As we entered, he bowed. Unfortunately when C. came into view he froze, and his mouth dropped open. There was quite a flutter. As she followed us up the aisle several of the villagers stood on their pews the better to get a glimpse of her. Children were lifted up, heads craned round the ends of the common pews, and such a rustling and exclaiming went on it was more like a fair than a church service.

Once C. had disappeared into our box she was no longer visible except for her feathers, which could clearly be seen above the partition. Mr Hunt was obliged to chide his parishioners in no uncertain terms before he could proceed with the service. 'We must remember,' he said, 'that we are all children of God, and though some of us may behave in a pagan manner, that does not mean there is no Christian heart beating underneath,' or words to that effect. C. stood up and bowed when he pointed at her and her gong clashed horribly. A few of our tenants tittered. All the tenants and farmers in Almondsbury are known to us, and the incident was really quite painful.

Mr Worrall, being the man he is, rose to the occasion magnificently, and read with such feeling I could not help but swell with pride.

C. paid great attention to the service, following the words in the prayer book with the tip of her finger and making little clicking noises as she attempted to mouth such strange characters. She appeared most devout during the prayers, and had to be induced to rise, for Allah Tallah apparently is worshipped at full length on the ground. It is a blessing she did not prostrate herself for there is so little room in the church. What *would* the congregation have thought?

Her gong boomed twice, but only faintly. The tambourine she laid beside me on the pew, intimating I could use it myself during the service if I so wished.

The Misses Amelia and Elizabeth Brooking did not wish us 'good morning' as we left the church. Old cats! I could see they were returning home hot foot to spread the news of C.'s appearance in church.

CHAPTER EIGHT

Caraboo is Painted and
Dr Wilkinson Appears on the Scene

MRS WORRALL'S DIARY
KNOLE PARK. MAY 16TH 1817

Mr Ponder of Cathay in the City of Bristol (a young pale gentleman wearing a watered silk waistcoat of bright pink) was here this morning. He has visited the Malay countries, he told me. He wished to meet C., hoping to throw some light on her language.

He brought with him a 'crease' (dagger) which C. immediately indicated was from Javasu. I could see from the animation of her expression, and the way she handled the weapon, that she was most anxious to keep it. 'Let me present it to her as a gift,' Mr Ponder implored me. 'She SO desires it, Ma'am.' I was adamant. 'Mr Ponder,' I told him, 'it is a dangerous weapon. She already fences with Mr Worrall using a stick; if she had this dagger, I fear Mr Worrall might be hurt.'

C. is so impulsive! So like a child! It is among her most endearing qualities; but I would not trust a child with a dagger.

Mr Ponder allowed C. to keep the dagger in her hand, though intimating to her that it was not hers, and must be returned to him.

C. walked about the room, feinting at imagined enemies, whirling about as though attacked from behind, and plunging the dagger high in the air in the manner of one killing birds.

'It is interesting to observe the Princess,' Mr Ponder remarked, 'for I see she has placed the dagger on the right side of her body. This is the custom of the Malay countries. In many other countries, the dagger is placed on the left.' However, Mr Ponder was unable to understand C.'s language. Such a disappointment! He was so full of hope when he arrived, and so pleased when he observed the position of the dagger.

'In the East,' Mr Ponder told me, 'the point of the dagger is stained with vegetable juice; a poison, Ma'am, which kills enemies on contact.'

I was only half listening to him, for to my amazement I observed Caraboo creep stealthily up on my jungle plant, and take a leaf between finger and thumb, rubbing the juice from thence onto the point of the dagger. 'Look!' I cried to Mr Ponder, 'see what Caraboo is doing!' Mr Ponder and I stopped talking, the better to watch C.

Having rubbed a great quantity of sticky sap from the leaf onto the tip of the dagger, she applied the point to her arm, scarcely grazing it – BUT THEN LOOKED AS THOUGH IN PAIN AND PRETENDED TO SWOON!

She could NOT have heard Mr Ponder tell me of this habit of Eastern people, for she was quite the other side of the room when he mentioned it to me. Also, how could she understand what he meant, when she knows so little English?

'We have a clue to her origins, here, Ma'am!' cried Mr Ponder, grasping me by the arm. 'Mr Ponder, we KNOW C. to be from the East,' I replied rather tartly, 'it is the exact place, not the general direction, we wish to ascertain.'

MRS WORRALL'S DIARY
KNOLE PARK. MAY 17TH 1817

Mr Bird, the most noted artist in Bristol, today offered to paint C. – for nothing! He waved aside my offer of fifty guineas for, he tells me, he will be honoured to welcome C. to his house. He feels she will add lustre to his name and interest to his studio.

I asked C. 'Would she like to be painted?' At first she understood this to mean, in the sense of war paint for the face! She took some charcoal from the fire and rubbed it across her cheeks, laughing at me as she did so (what large expressive eyes she has, they are so full of sensibility!) When I pointed to the picture of Mr Worrall's grandfather above the fireplace and told her THAT was the type of painting we had in mind, she pulled a great face, apeing Mr Worrall's grandfather to the life – making her own face quite ugly, and somehow creating the impression of whiskers and a beard, I know not how. When I laughed aloud, she clapped her hands together and pirouetted on her heel. She was delighted with the idea.

I explained Mr Bird had suggested we visit the studio in the afternoon, and she ran to dress herself up in her finery, begging the loan of a rope of pearls from me. This, she felt, would complete her Javasu costume. I was happy to lend them to her.

News somehow spread that C. and I were coming to Bristol for C.'s portrait to be painted. Crowds lined the street to the studio, and as we descended from the carriage a voice called out 'Three cheers for the Princess Caraboo!' C. glanced around as tho' used to such admiration, and salaamed the crowd. At once a great roar of appreciation went up. I was SO proud.

Mr Bird was waiting for us in the studio, a large airy room with much of his work on display. I particularly noted a naked female, almost life size. This, Mr Bird told me, was Andromache. I wonder who this Andromache is. I must ask Mr Worrall.

We had scarcely time to look round the studio before Mr Bird announced he had assembled several of the most important patrons of the arts of the city of Bristol, whom he wished to introduce to C. and myself.

C. has such natural elegance! When introduced to each person in turn as 'The Princess Caraboo', she salaamed with the utmost ease of manner. She of course, took the title for granted. I, I own, was flattered at such respect shown to my protégée. Her graceful movements contrasted SO strongly with the dry old sticks of patrons, who positively staggered with age. They were completely won by her charms. She has such white teeth when she laughs! I fear my own teeth are decaying. I felt a twinge from the back molar again today.

After the introductions C. was told to move freely about the studio. She darted happily among the canvases and paints, with such childlike enthusiasm I feared she would upset Mr Bird's carefully contrived still-life, of pheasants, apples and a hare. He told me it was to be called 'An Autumn Morning'. The birds were so dead I am surprised they had not rotted away. The apples were speckled with mildew. I held my handkerchief to my nose. I do hope Mr Bird did not notice. Perhaps he has no sense of smell?

At length Mr Bird dismissed the company and brought a chair for me, which he set down behind his easel, so that I could watch him at work. C. was placed on a dais and arranged looking over her shoulder, three-quarter face, with a delightful mischievous expression. 'She looks somewhat like Lady Hamilton,' said Mr Bird, 'one of the greatest beauties of our time. But the Princess has more MYSTERY about her.' I thrilled at his words.

Mr Bird sketched the face and posture very rapidly (so interesting) and told us he would fill in the background later. There was no necessity for C. to sit for him more than half a dozen times.

I am so pleased there is to be a portrait of Caraboo. Future generations will be able to judge her rare quality for themselves.

Dr C.H. Wilkinson *Bath City Record Office*

Letter from Dr Charles Hunnings Wilkinson of
Burlington Street, Bath
to Mrs Worrall of Knole Park
May 17th 1817

Madam,

    We are not yet acquainted but I feel – if you will excuse the liberty – that I know you well, having heard so much of your benevolence and the humane attentions you bestow on the mysterious stranger who but recently entered Almondsbury in search of shelter. Your name, Madam, is on the lips of all Bath. We wait in eager anticipation to hear the latest news from Knole.

    Let me introduce myself Madam. I am a scientist, of whom you may have heard. I can converse in several languages. My essays on Galvanism have

46

not, I venture to believe, gone unnoticed and my 'Elements of Galvanism in theory and practice', dedicated to Sir Joseph Banks, received some acclaim. In the medical application of Galvanism I believe no person in England has been more extensively engaged than myself. During recent experiments I devised a Battery consisting of fifty three-inch plates, useful for either philosophical or medical purposes and available from me at a cost of five guineas for use in affections of the head, tooth-ache and ear-ache, gutta serena, impotence, deafness, asthma, paralysis and other complaints. But I digress.

You may also have heard of me Madam, as the Proprietor of the Pump Room Baths, which have been considerably enlarged since they came into my possession. I look forward to welcoming you there one day. Every Monday and Friday I deliver a series of practical talks, at precisely one-o-clock, on the different branches of Experimental Philosophy, chemistry and mineralogy. I also give private talks to families of not less than six, during which I allow them to experiment themselves. There is no danger in it.

You may have guessed why I am writing to you and telling you so much about myself. I beg you, as a man deeply involved in all aspects of scientific marvels, to allow me the privilege of calling upon you and the Princess Caraboo. Such an honour would give me so much pleasure!

I would like the opportunity to talk with her alone, if this is possible – save for your own presence, of course, Madam.

I await your reply in great eagerness of spirit. Do not deny me this favour. Should I be the one to discover her language, Madam, my joy would know no bounds!

I am, Madam,
Yr. obed. hmble svt.
C.H.Wilkinson

*Letter from Mrs Worrall of Knole Park
to Dr Wilkinson, Pump Rooms, Bath
May 19th 1817*

Dear Dr Wilkinson,
Your letter was of the greatest fascination and I look forward to the pleasure of meeting you. I have told Princess Caraboo (as best I can under the circumstances) of your many accomplishments and she, likewise, is eager to make your acquaintance.

Early in the morning is the only time we can guarantee no visitors – about nine of the clock is suitable. Would tomorrow be a possibility?

I have a bothersome tooth which is afflicting me quite dreadfully with the Tooth Ache at the moment. I only tell you this, for fear you might think me rude, were I to look unwelcoming on your arrival.

I remain, sir,

etc.

Elizabeth Worrall

Letter from Mrs Worrall of Knole Park
to Jane Worsthorn of Stony Easton Lodge
May 22nd 1817

Dearest J.

Such a day! Dr Wilkinson came to visit – did I mention Dr W. when I last saw you? He is the proprietor of the Pump Room at Bath. Did you meet him when you took water there? He is a little, plump, verbose man, wearing an old-fashioned stock, with his hair tied back in a queue.

He has been MOST insistent he come here, to meet C. ON HIS OWN! He stipulated no other visitors must be present. It was very difficult to arrange so we decided on early morning, before our many visitors arrive.

He is such a dear, good man. He had on a green coat with a red brocade waistcoat, and carried with him his portable Galvanic Battery.

I had woken in the morning with a recurrence of my Tooth Ache. Mr Worrall has peered into my mouth and pronounced it a tooth gone rotten. I knew the monster must be pulled. Your receipt for Tooth Ache DID NOT WORK, Jane. I became drowsy and light headed after the morphia. Often I slept, but afterwards the pain returned with greater force.

When Dr W. arrived C. was bathing my forehead with eau-de-cologne. I was prostrate on the couch.

At once Dr W. sensed my distress. 'Allow me, Madam,' he said 'This will cure the Tooth Ache once and for all, but you must be BRAVE.' He took my hand and laid in it a cable, not the thickness of a finger, which led from his machine. Having greeted C. he then asked her to turn the handle of the machine. This she did.

I felt such strange sensations, such a prickling and tingling of the skin, and in fright I nearly let go of the cable. Dr W. INSISTED I continue holding it while opening my mouth for him to see inside. Suddenly I felt a tweek – and then the pain was GONE! Dr W. had produced a pair of forceps from somewhere about his person, and, locating the offending tooth – pulled! I was conscious only of the new electricity on my hand. I felt nothing!

Dr W. held up the tooth for me to see. Such a small, black thing to have caused so much trouble!

Dr W. says electricity shows great promise as a cure-all for most diseases. He has been using it in his clinic in London, where beds are connected to the machines. Dr W. also believes in the curative powers of gases. In his clinic a room is fitted up with pipes, down which gases flow to his patients lined up in beds.

He is so interesting! What a remarkable man. We are lucky having him so near us, in Bath.

He spent the greater part of the day with us, reading the letters I have received about C., and Capt. Palmer's notes, and conversing with C. He was CHARMED with C. He could not take his eyes off her. There were not so many visitors today, so she danced for Dr W. and made quite a fuss of him.

He is writing to the *Bath Chronicle* about C. If this brings no results, he hopes to take her to India House, to see the Directors there.

In the meantime we have between us written a letter to Oxford University, addressed to Mr Coplestone and to the Rev. Whalley, whom he knows. We have included in the pacquet samples of C.'s writing, and some drawings of her travels.

Jane – I told you, did I not, of Bertha Tiddles, my dairymaid? I have dismissed her, and she has gone to an Aunt, for her mother is not pleased with her. Today Reuben Slaughter, one of the gardeners, comes to me, asking me where she is gone, he is the father of her child – she has written him a note to tell him so. He wishes to marry her and her mother will not say where she is.

This SAME AFTERNOON, some two hours later, comes a knock on the door and in marches Farrar, the new under footman, to tell me HE is the father of Bertha's child, and she has written to tell HIM so and he will marry her!

I sent a message post haste to Bertha asking her to come and see me. What shall I do?

Affect.
Elizabeth

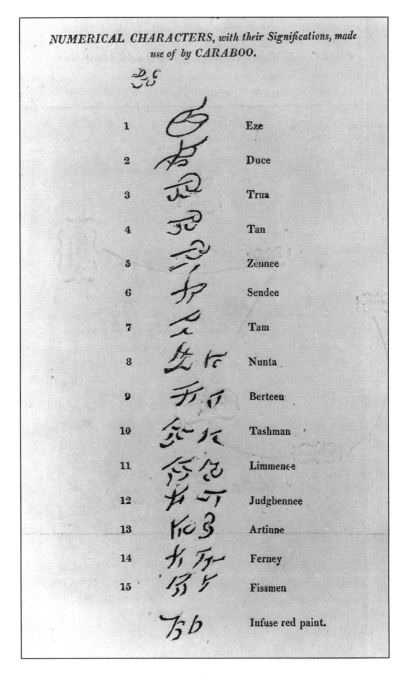

NUMERICAL CHARACTERS, *with their Significations, made use of by* CARABOO.

1		Eze
2		Duce
3		Trua
4		Tan
5		Zennee
6		Sendee
7		Tam
8		Nunta
9		Berteen
10		Tashman
11		Limmenee
12		Judgbennee
13		Artinne
14		Ferney
15		Fissmen
		Infuse red paint.

Caraboo's Numerical Characters *British Library*

Letter from Jane Worsthorn of Stony Easton Lodge
to Mrs Worrall of Knole Park
May 23rd, 10 a.m.

Dear E.,
Do nothing. The girl is FAST.

Affect.
Jane

Letter from Mrs Worrall of Knole Park
to Jane Worsthorn of Stony Easton Lodge
May 23rd, 4 p.m.

Jane,
Bertha came this afternoon. I taxed her with her two love-sick swains, and asked which was the father of her child. She said she did not know. I asked her which one she wished to marry? She told me, neither, she hoped for a better, but the child needed a father.

I asked, would she see them, to tell them her decision? She said, if I wished.

I am sorry for Farrar, who is a nice young man, and well mannered. To be saddled with such a baggage as this, for all her blue eyes and flaxen hair, and her way with the cows. Reuben, I do not know. His widowed mother was servant to Lady Cecil of Bath, and recommended to me.

Your letter has been no help.

Affect.
E.

CHAPTER NINE

Caraboo's Disappearance and Illness

MRS WORRALL'S DIARY
MAY 25TH 1817

C. vanished from the house two days ago, leaving us a prey to all manner of anxieties. She returned in the evening (when we had scoured the neighbourhood) covered in mud, blistered and so tired she could scarcely stand.

I was so upset by her appearance I did not like to ask her where she had been or what she had done. Mrs Pike later told me that she had been to dig up her clothes, which she had hidden in a field, to keep them from the Macratoos!

I confess, I eyed her bundles with interest; but when we looked inside, there was only a print gown, cottage bonnet and shawl. Not garments that could have come from Javasu; more probably, the clothes that she exchanged for her own on landing here.

She was burning with fever when she came to see me in the evening. Her forehead was damp with heat and her eyes staring. Mrs Pike put her to bed with the help of Stephens, and for several days we feared she would die. I have been so worried I have been unable to write.

Mr Mortimer came from Bristol. He is such a clever surgeon! I felt only he could save C. He pronounced it to be the ordinary fever, one that comes and goes, and is prevalent in the Spring. Fearing he might be wrong, we called in two medical men from Bath who saw her and confirmed his opinion.

I cannot forgive one Mr Sawbones for what he did. He appeared to think this a good moment to test C. (How can they still doubt C? It is Monstrous!) He turned to me (and my feelings can be imagined) and said, in a penetrating voice 'The Princess Caraboo is in extreme danger. It is probable she will not last the night.'

How DARE he frighten us in such a manner?

C. became very crimson in the face at these words. Mrs Pike says her temperature rises and falls to an alarming degree, and in the evening her colour comes and goes with peculiar rapidity. Stephens, who is devotedly attending C. told clever Mr Sawbones that such flushing took place six or seven times a day since the start of C.'s fever. It is a common occurrence in this type of fever. However, for several minutes we DID wonder if C. had understood his remark.

C. was bled to bring her temperature down to normal and at length she recovered. Never, even when at the POINT OF DEATH, did she speak any other language but her own.

How can anyone doubt her, now?

Peterson has just come in. He is full of apologies for ever doubting C. He assures me he will treat her with the greatest respect and gentleness now that she is recovered, and help look after her until she is fully on her feet again.

Letter from Dr C.H. Wilkinson of Burlington St, Bath
to the Editor of the Bath Chronicle
June 1st, 1817

Sir,

The present inexplicable appearance of a young female foreigner in the vicinity of Bristol, having excited considerable curiosity and as I have had the opportunity of being in her company, and of obtaining what information is at present known, from her benevolent protectress, Mrs W. of Knole, at whose house she resides, I am desired to request you will be so obliging as to insert these particulars in your Chronicle, with the hope that they will be copied into many provincial papers. So that by such a general dissemination they may be read by some who have observed a female, corresponding to the description here given, and may ultimately lead to the development of those circumstances, which have placed a most interesting female in a truly distressing situation.

I am, Sir,
Your's,
C.H. WILKINSON

About two months since, a female presented herself at the door of a cottage at Almondsbury, near Bristol. The door being open and a couch in view, she made signs of a wish to repose herself. She appeared in a very debilitated and distressed condition, as if exhausted by much fatigue. The cottagers, not

Princess Caraboo of Javasu, 1817 after the engraving by Edward Bird
City of Bristol Museum & Art Gallery

Engraving of Mary Wilcox of Witheridge, Devonshire alias Caraboo
British Library

comprehending her language, reported the case to Mrs W. who resides about a mile from Almondsbury, and that lady kindly visited, and gave orders for the most humane attention to be paid to her. Her language was equally unknown to Mrs W. but her appearance and graceful manners so interested that lady, that she took her under her own roof, where she has since experienced the most unremitting kindness. Her head is small, her eyes and hair are black, her eye-brows finely arched, the forehead low and nose rather short. Her complexion is very trifling sallow, rather more corresponding to a brunette, with a pleasing colour on the cheeks. A sweet smile, her mouth rather large with beautifully white and regular teeth and lips a little prominent and full, the under lip rather projecting. Her chin is small and round. No ear-rings, but marks of having worn them, and hands unaccustomed to labour. In height five feet two inches. Her dress consisted of a black stuff gown, with a muslin frill round the neck, a black cotton shawl on the head, and a red and black one around the shoulders, leather shoes and black worsted stockings. She appears to be about 25 years of age. Her manners are extremely graceful, her countenance of surprising fascination.

Such is the general effect on all who behold her, that, if before she had been suspected as an impostor, the sight of her removes all doubt. Her mode of diet seems to be Hindoostanic, as she lives principally on vegetables, and is very partial to curry. She will occasionally take fish, but no other animal food. Water is her beverage, and she expresses great disgust at the appearance of wine, spirits, or any other intoxicating liquors. Whatever she eats, she prepares herself. She is extremely neat in her attire and is very cautious in her conduct with respect to gentlemen, never allowing them to take hold of her hand, and retiring from them. When she takes leave of a gentleman, it is by the application of the right hand to the right side of the forehead, and, in like manner, on taking leave of a lady, she does the same with the left hand.

She appears to be devout and on a certain day in the week is anxious to go to the top of the house, there to pay adoration to the sun from the rising to the setting. She casually saw a dagger and, as if anxious to inform her kind patroness of all the customs of her country, which she calls JAVASU, she placed the dagger to her right side. She fences with great dexterity, holding the sword in her right hand and the dagger in her left. She is very fond of bathing and swims and dives with considerable activity. She carries about with her a cord, on which some knots are made, like the Chinese *abacus*, which afterwards gave rise to the sliding beads, the SUON PUON. She writes with great facility from left to right, as we are accustomed. She had made Mrs W. understand that in her country neither pens nor paper are used, but what is supposed to be a camel hair pencil and a species of papyrus.

Soon after her residence in Mrs W.'s house, she was attacked with a

CHARACTERS made use of by CARABOO, and her AUTOGRAPH of MARY BAKER.

☞ The lettered reader will perceive a few perfectly-formed and conjoined Arabic characters; it need not to be added, that she copied them from those which some Oriental Scholar wrote before her..

* Allah Tallah.

Caraboo's alphabet and the signature of Mary Baker *British Library*

typhus fever, and was placed under the care of Mr Mortimer, an eminent surgeon of Bristol. Upon her recovery, pleased as she must have been at his kind and constant attention to her, she wrote him a letter of thanks, calling him, as a doctor, JUSTEE, and herself CARABOO.

All the assistance to be derived from a Polyglott Bible, Fry's 'Pantographia', or Dr Hager's 'Elementary Characters of the Chinese', do not enable us to ascertain either the nature of her language, or the country to which she belongs. One or two characters bear some resemblance to the Chinese, particularly CHO, a reed; there are more characters which have some similitude to the Greek, particularly ξ, π, Γ; different publications have been shewn to her, in Greek, Malay, Chinese, Sanscrit, Arabic and Persic, but with all she appears entirely unacquainted. Her letter has been shewn to every person in Bristol and Bath versed in oriental literature, but without success. A copy was sent to the India-House, and submitted by the chairman of that company to the attention of Mr RAFFLES, one of the best oriental scholars, yet he could not decypher it. The original letter was sent to Oxford, and the members of that University denied it being the character of any language. Others have supposed it to be in the style of the Malay of Sumatra. From my own observations, although entirely unacquainted with any single character of her writing, I have deemed her more resembling the Circassian. Her countenance, her complexion and her manners favour such a supposition, and probably her appearance here may be connected with the Corsairs who have been hovering about our coast. She has by signs intimated that she was on board a ship, and so ill-treated, that when she came within sight of land, she jumped overboard and swam ashore. She also, in the same manner, expressed that she was ill on board, her hair cut off, and an operation on the back performed. I examined the part, it had been scarified, but not according to the English mode of cupping, or to any European manner with which I am acquainted. The incisions are extremely regular, and apparently employed with the caustic, a mode of cupping adopted in the East.

The Supreme Being she styles 'Allah Tallah'.

All who have seen her are highly interested about her. A fac-simile of her letter is being placed in the Kingston Pump-Room, for examination. I beg leave to observe that I have seen her write, and she writes with grace and facility.

P.S. Since writing the above, I have been informed of the following circumstances. CARABOO quitted Mrs W.'s house for one whole day, to procure a few clothes, which she signified to Mrs W. that she had buried, to conceal them from the MACRATOOS (rogues). The distance must have been considerable, as her feet were blistered, and the violent illness which followed was owing to the fatigue. Mrs W., whose opportunities of observing her have necessarily been superior to those of any other person, is persuaded her father is Chinese, and that her mother, who is dead, was Malay; that her father's name is *Jessee Mandu*, and that he is a man of considerable consequence in his own country. CARABOO describes a gold chain he wears about his neck.

Letter from Ambrose Browning
to Mrs Worrall of Knole Park
Edinburgh. June 3rd 1817

Mrs Worrall, Madam,

I wish to be excused for making so bold as to trouble you with a letter, making a few inquiries respecting the female foreigner, whom, being destitute, you have so kindly, humanely and generously sheltered under your hospitable roof. I have carefully read the description of her given in various Scottish publications, and the supposition that she is a Circassian (as I myself was brought up in that country) makes me particularly anxious to know about her.

Her features, food, mode of eating, the caution in her conduct with respect to gentlemen, the use she makes of her hands in taking leave of ladies and gentlemen, her disgust at wine, spirits, and intoxicating liquors; all favour Dr Wilkinson's opinion. Her mode of worship, too, on the house top with her face towards the east, resembles that of the Circassians, were it not that she pays adoration to the sun. The Circassions worship and pay adoration to none other but the true God, facing Mecca. They are under the impression that, on their Prophet Mahomet's account, the Author of all things on earth makes that spot his chief abode. The God they worship they call Allah-Tallah. It is probable the female foreigner, in this respect, may be misunderstood. Instead of worshipping the sun, she, like them, may, with her face towards Mecca, worship the same God (as it evidently appears from her giving God the same name Allah-Tallah, by interpretation, God Almighty). If thus misunderstood, her mode of worship likewise supports the idea that she is a Circassian.

There are, however, other things which make her being a Circassian doubtful. I do not recollect ever seeing a Circassian female wearing a BLACK STUFF GOWN WITH A MUSLIN FRILL ROUND HER NECK, as this is a continental fashion. The WORSTED STOCKINGS, also, to the best of my knowledge are no part of Circassian dress, but these articles have not been made sufficiently plain, and a description of the clothes she afterwards bought has been wholly omitted.

The next most doubtful of all is her writing. All the while I was in Circassia, I neither saw nor heard of more than two of their women being capable of writing, and even those wrote with an Arabic character from right to left. But she is said to write from left to right, with a character as yet unknown, and that with great facility.

I am unacquainted with any of the names Javasu, Malay, Jessee Mandu and Caraboo, as applied, though some of their parts may have meaning, either in Tartar of in Circassian. The part Java, of the name Javasu, in Circassian, may either signify a surface of any thing, or the second person imperative mode of the verb TO DRINK. The latter part, SU, signifies WATER in Tartar. The part MAL of the name MALAY, signifies SHEEP in Circassian. The other, AY, is an interjection in Tartar and in Circassian, of the same meaning as in English. The first part JESSEE in the name JESSEE MANDU, in Tartar signifies AN OWNER. To the last part I can give no signification. The first part of the name CARA, is either a Tartar adjective signifying BLACK, or the second person imperative mood of the Tartar verb TO LOOK. The last part BOO, signifying THIS OR THAT, is a pronoun in the same language.

It will not be improper here to observe that by the name alone it is impossible to know a Circassian, names being given at random, made of words in two or three languages, and often of none at all.

Having stated the reasons for my thinking her a CIRCASSIAN, and those which make me doubtful, I shall now, in ROMAN CHARACTERS, set down a few questions in the Circassian and Tartar languages, which being carefully read to her, by the observation of the rules given, may lead to a discovery whether she be a Circassian or a Tartar.

Rule for the Circassian questions
Sound all the letters as in English, the vowel 'a' as in FAT, 'u' as in FULL, and 'g' hard before 'e' and 'i'. Along with the questions I set down a translation.

Circassian
1st. ADIGIVZAR UPTSHERA? Do you understand Circassian?
2nd. UADIGA? Are you a Circassian?
3rd. SET ETSH UKYKA? What land do you come from?
4th. UI YADER ADIGIT? Was your father a Circassian?
5th. ETSAR SETIT? What was his name?
6th. UI YANER ADIGIT? Was your mother a Circassian?
7th. UI TSHEMA ETSAR SET? What is the name of your country?
8th. ADIGIVZER UPTSHAMA, EGE UNJESSA PESSELTHAHEMA JUAP KUZAT? If you understand the Circassian language, give an answer to the words now spoken.
NOTE: Sound 'u' in the last word, as in URN.

Rule for the Tartar questions
Sound 'a' again as in FAT, the dipthong 'oi' as in OIL, 'e' marked $\tilde{e}$ as in ME, ĕ marked thus 'e' as in Eden, 'g' hard before 'e', as formerly.

1st. NOGOI TILLEN BĒLLASĔNMA? Do you understand the Tartar language?

2nd. NOGI SĔNMA? Are you a Tartar?

3rd. NEĔ JERDEN SHUKHANSEN? From what land are you?

4th. ATANG NOGOI ĒDĔMA? Was your father a Tartar?

5th. ATA NĔ ĔDĔ? What was his name?

6th. ANANG NOGOI PĔSHY ĔDĔMA? Was your mother a Tartar woman?

7th. SĔNUNG JĔRUNGNUNG ATA NĒDĒR? What is the name of your country?

8th. EGĔR NOGOI TILLDA BĒLLZUNG, SORRAHAN? HUMHA JUAB BĔR? If you understand the Tartar language, answer the questions asked you.

NOTE: Sound the 'u' in SHUKHANSEN (3rd question) as in LUCK.

I hope the above will afford some degree of satisfaction, but if she understands none of the above sentences I have set down, her giving the Supreme Being the name ALLAH-TALLAH will be a wonder to me, being a Circassian word, and one familiar to me.

Have the goodness to send me an answer to this letter, with a description of all her clothes, some of the characters she writes, and a few words of the language she speaks, and, if a Circassian, her answers to the questions I have given.

Thus you will oblige your humble servant,
A.B.

MRS WORRALL'S DIARY
KNOLE PARK. FRIDAY JUNE 6TH 1817

Today has been most unpleasant. Cold wind and heavy rain made worse by the disappearance of C. Again! My feelings on discovering her gone have been those of great unease. Though she is well again, she is not STRONG. Mrs Pike and I discovered not a pin nor a ribbon missing. Her bundle, though, containing a few necessaries, has disappeared. I am almost out of my mind with worry. Do I look after her well enough? Has her illness made her restless and eager to return to Javasu?

The day was made worse by the delivery of a pacquet from Oxford University, containing C.'s writing and the map we had drawn of her voyage. The letter, enclosed, claims that C.'s language is the 'Hum Bug' language. I do not know what they mean. I shall ask Dr Wilkinson when I next see him.

Will Frogley has just come in search of me, to tell me that fool of a blacksmith has lamed Belmont. Again! He is always the worse for liquor. I MUST try to find another Blacksmith, but it is so difficult, for there is so much rivalry in the village. Will Frogley turned his back for only a moment during the shoeing, and that fool smith struck the nail at the wrong angle.

We searched and called for C., but with no effect. Mr Worrall had already left for the Bank when we discovered C. gone. Mr Worrall is so pale and silent these days. He has not mentioned the Bank again, but I feel uneasy.

I sent Will Frogley to Jane (W) as we thought C. might have gone there, but Will returned alone, and without news.

Why did she go? Where has she gone? Jane thinks she has gone to look for a boat for Javasu, anxious to see her family again. Jane has ridden over to help in the search and to comfort me. I am MUCH in need of it. I asked Jane, 'Would she go without saying farewell?' (To me.) Jane is of the opinion C. is still a savage at heart and does not heed our formalities.

We searched and called for C. all afternoon. I sent Will to ask the village boys to look in all the trees. Eleven of our servants are out hunting for C. I hear voices everywhere calling 'Caraboo'. At dusk we took the lanterns out to continue the search. Has she been injured? Abducted? There is no knowing what may have befallen her.

Mrs Pike asked cook to make my favourite dish, a concoction of veal and spinage, with gooseberry pie to follow. I felt quite unable to do justice to the dishes, though Jane stayed for supper and Mr Worrall returned from the Bank in time to eat heartily. Can he be unwell if his appetite is so good?

I retired to bed early, tossing and turning the night through. My head aches as I write this, in the early morning. The grey dawn light is filtering through the trees of the park. What will tomorrow bring? Is Caraboo hiding somewhere? Have her strange ways landed her in gaol?

MRS WORRALL'S DIARY
KNOLE PARK. SUNDAY JUNE 8TH 1817, A.M.

Two days have passed. I have scarcely slept nor ate. No sign of C. until this morning early, a message came from Dr Wilkinson, informing us C. in Bath! How she got there we do not know. Why did she not get in touch with me? Why leave so suddenly? These questions will, I hope, soon be answered.

Mr Worrall says he will not accompany me to Bath. He is busy with the Bank. STILL worried about money, I am sure. My yellow velvet spencer a mistake, Mr Worrall says. Too expensive. I tell him the price has risen between the ordering and the making, and it will last for years. Mr Worrall says he has heard THAT before. My new carriage hat with plumes arrives tomorrow. How CAN I tell Mr Worrall?

Jane (W) also says she cannot come to Bath. The chestnut mare (Kitty) is due to foal and needs constant attention. Two grooms and various stable boys are hovering around. Such a fuss! Now she must needs borrow Will Frogley. Not a long 'borrowing' she says but I inform her I need him for my journey to Bath.

I am to set off alone in the chaise.

Damp and chilly weather, and the road will be bad. I am in a fever of anxiety. What is C. doing? Who is taking care of her?

7.p.m.

I *cannot* describe the scene that met me in Bath.

I had already been informed of C.'s whereabouts by Dr Wilkinson, and was readily admitted to the house, a large stone mansion set back from the street. A line of females waited patiently upon the staircase, I could not think what FOR.

I passed them without thinking.

I burst into the drawing room and what a sight met my eyes! C. was seated on a – I can only describe it as a THRONE. (A red velvet cloak thrown over an armchair.) A string of ladies stood before her, waiting to be introduced. This was the reason for the queue. She appeared totally at her ease. Two ladies knelt at her feet. One held her hand and whispered to her, the other begged a kiss. A third was behind her, in the act of putting a string of pearls round C.'s neck.

The moment I burst in, C. looked up. The instant she recognised me she fell to her knees. Such complete prostration moved me almost to tears. She embraced me with such an ardour of attachment I saw moisture in every eye. Several ladies sobbed. C.'s face expressed such JOY at my appearance I began to doubt my senses. Why had she left, if she cared so much for me? Did sudden homesickness overcome her? I *could* not help but forgive her the anxiety she had caused me.

Suddenly – C. DASHED FROM THE ROOM!

I feared I had lost her again. My heart began to beat very fast and the ladies turned to each other asking 'where is she going? Why has she fled? etc. etc.' I had only *one* thought in mind; to pursue her, and persuade her to explain the meaning of her conduct. I found her in the parlour. She made signs that she needed to be alone with me to make me understand WHY she had disappeared.

It was as Jane and I had suspected. She had left Knole ONLY because the anxiety to find her family had grown too much for her. Nothing else would have induced her to leave. Her expressions of sorrow at my evident distress were so moving I had difficulty restraining my tears.

Tonight I am more convinced THAN EVER that C. is indeed the Princess she says that she is. If *only* we could find her island and restore her to her father!

We returned to Knole together. C. looked so happy! She called Knole 'home'. The first time I have heard her use that word.

Later
I met Dr Wilkinson on the road. He tells me that one gentleman was so persuaded of C.'s plight he offered to subscribe £500 to send her home to whatever island it was discovered she was from. A collection of money was at once started, and notes strewn on the table (I had noticed them, but thought nothing of it, assuming that someone had been gambling). C. showed the utmost nonchalance when faced with the money, she even attempted to tear a few notes in half, for sport! Of course, to her they are but sheets of paper!

Letter from Dr Charles Hunnings Wilkinson of Burlington St, Bath to the Editor of the Bath Chronicle
June 9th 1817

Last Saturday evening, about seven o'clock, CARABOO arrived at the Pack-Horse Inn in this city. It appeared that the driver of a caravan invited her to ride, and about three miles distant from Bristol, on the road to Bath, she got into the vehicle but would not admit of any assistance from the driver.

When brought to the above Inn, considerable embarrassment was experienced from the inability of comprehending her language, but the landlady paid the kindest attentions to her, and at length comprehended her wish, FROM HER DELINEATING A TREE, WHICH WAS CONJEC-TURED TO BE THE TEA TREE.

The arrival of the stranger under these circumstances soon excited considerable attention, and particularly that of a gentleman, a Mr Carpenter, who, having a few minutes before read the account given in our last Chronicle, supposed this person to be the one described, and in conse-quence sent information of her to me.

I received it too late to visit her that evening, but between seven and eight o'clock the next morning I went to the Inn, and found CARABOO at breakfast with the landlady. She immediately recognised me, and I adopted those measures which would the most expeditiously intimate her situation to her kind patroness, Mrs W.

As soon as breakfast was finished, Caraboo disappeared. I followed her, and casually met her alone in the Circus. She walked about for some time, and then returned to the Inn, where she readily followed me into the dining room, and I left her in charge of a female in the house.

About twelve o'clock, it appeared that public curiosity would be considerably excited, and that probably CARABOO would be annoyed by many visitors. Two ladies, who had been sitting by her for sometime, and who experienced pity for an interesting female, thrown, by circumstances as yet unknown, on a country where the inhabitants and the language were equally strange to her (those feelings which shew in the most inestimable point of view the human mind) offered the protection of their house in Russell Street, and thither CARABOO was immediately removed in a chair. Her confidence, by the kind treatment she received, was soon excited. Her countenance became animated with smiles of gratitude and she endeavoured to explain to the ladies THE CUSTOMS OF HER COUNTRY, BY ACTIONS THE MOST GRACEFUL, AND BY MANNERS HIGHLY FASCINATING!

In the evening, her benevolent protectress appeared. Immediately on the sight of her, the situation of CARABOO – the graceful manner in which she prostrated herself to solicit pardon for having left Mrs W.'s house – most sensibly affected every person present. Upon enquiry, it appears that CARABOO, anxiously wishing to return home to her father, her husband and her child, thought this could sooner be accomplished by her removal to some other place.

All the circumstances attending her leaving Knole evinced a mind formed on the most correct principles of honour. Various little articles and trinkets which had been presented to her, also money in a purse, were all left in the greatest order in her room, and she quitted Knole without a single farthing in her pocket.

Upon every occasion she has shown great dignity of mind. Her astonishing power of interesting all around her appeared most satisfactorily, in the great interest excited in the truly amiable mind of her protectress.

When CARABOO'S absence was ascertained, Mrs W.'s anxiety was indescribable. Ten or twelve persons were sent in different directions to find her and as soon as the intimation arrived of her being in BATH, the carriage was immediately directed to the same place.

Every circumstance which has transpired since my last communication, contributes to the proof that Caraboo is the character she represents herself to be, and those who have paid the greatest attention to her have no doubt that she is a native of one of the Japanese islands, called Javasu, and that her father is Chinese. From some circumstances it would appear that her mother was of European descent, probably Portugese. She is evidently acquainted with the principles of Christianity, as she described the crucifixion and resurrection.

What has been reported of a similar female having been seen at Cork, upon inquiry, turns out incorrect. NOTHING HAS YET TRANSPIRED TO AUTHORISE THE SLIGHTEST SUSPICION OF CARABOO, NOR HAS SUCH EVER BEEN ENTERTAINED, EXCEPT BY THOSE WHOSE SOULS FEEL NOT THE SPIRIT OF BENEVOLENCE, AND WISH TO CONVERT TO RIDICULE THAT AMIABLE DISPOSITION IN OTHERS!

It ought to be remarked that, from the indefatigable attention of Capt. Palmer, and from the Journal of Mrs W., a more correct account of this surprisingly interesting female may be expected.

C.H. Wilkinson

CHAPTER TEN

The Unmasking

A strange unpleasant incident took place this morning. I do not know *what* to make of it. C. came to my dressing room, as usual, to watch me dress and help brush my hair. She lays out the jewellery she wishes me to wear, and agrees with Stephens the garments I am to put on. It is always a most amusing occasion.

Today she entered the room and TURNED THE KEY IN THE LOCK. She closed the door on Stephens, who had gone to fetch my lace fichu.

I looked at her in surprise. She held the key in her hand, as though weighing it. Moving close to me she played with the combs and brushes on my dressing table. I said nothing, but observed her closely. She looked dispirited and near to tears, as though she had something AWFUL to tell me. Twice she approached me and opened her mouth, but no sound came from it.

'What is it, Caraboo?' I said at last, as gently as I was able for the fearful fluttering of my nerves. She smiled then, and, hearing Stephens' footsteps approach, unlocked the door (as though it had been a mere whim) and made a deep salaam. For an instant I thought she would kiss the hem of my dress, as in the past. What can this mean? My heart is heavy when I remember the incident.

I wished to hear what Will Frogley thought of Bertha Tiddles, and mentioned her name to him this morning. He shook his head and looked MOST severe for Will. 'She'll come to no good, Ma'am,' he told me. 'She has EYES and a way with her.' I think I know what he means. There is a plague of rats in the stables and they are collecting terriers from the village for a ratting party. Will says the betting will be heavy, for Badger, old Tom's

67

terrier, has killed more than a thousand rats and is champion ratter of the neighbourhood. I shall keep Stumpy well out of the way.

Dr W. came to visit. I fear it was only to ascertain C. was safe and happy. He is devoted to her. I told him he was 'dressed to kill' (such an amusing expression) for he was wearing clothes suitable for a much younger man. They looked new. How C. has changed us all! A yellow broadcloth coat and Wellington boots are quite the fashion, he assures me, since the Battle of Waterloo. The boots do not let in the damp, and are very patriotic. It is rare to find a fashion that is both convenient and keeps out the wet.

He informs me the *Bath Chronicle* are reprinting his first letter about C. Also a second letter he sent recently. He has high hopes of the result.

I think only Dr W. can discover the truth about C. On Tuesday he plans to take her to London, to India House. I quite forgot to tell him the extraordinary answer I received from Oxford University about her writing.

MRS WORRALL'S DIARY
KNOLE PARK. JUNE 10TH, 4 P.M.

It is over. How could I have been so mistaken? C. is an impostor. She is the daughter of a cobbler from somewhere in the West country. Tears are falling on this page as I write. Can I be angry? I wish I COULD be angry with C. I have become so fond of her I do believe I forgive her even this. I shall burn this Journal. How ridiculous it seems to think it would be of interest. I feel the last few weeks have been a mockery. But C. did not laugh. She was trapped by her own cleverness and by her desire to please.

Mr Worrall tells me I have been sentimental and romantic. He says the troubles at the Bank have kept him from putting a stop to this 'charade'. But he fenced with her! He enjoyed her company! She amused him, and relaxed him when he was upset from his day at the Bank. She danced for him in the evenings and I told him her latest 'exploits' and so made him laugh. He always said it was like a Play. Now he says I am too ready to be taken advantage of, too gullible, too – stupid – but he refrained from saying so.

I shall never wear the turban with the gold feathers. I have not the heart for it. It was vastly expensive.

Mr Worrall tells me he was ALWAYS suspicious of C. He adds he found her delightful to be with, such fun and so amusing. That makes me feel a little better.

He says (now) that her fencing could have been learnt with sticks on the village green – her quickness of eye and foot make her excellent, not her manner of doing. Also her swimming – many villagers swim from an early age if near a river or pond. It is self-taught, and the mothers are keen they should learn, so that they should not drown.

News today that Bertha Tiddles has run off with a Gypsy from an encampment nearby. Her mother is FURIOUS with the Aunt for not keeping better watch on her.

How the Misses Brooking will crow over me! They were always jealous.

Letter from Mrs Worrall of Knole Park
to Jane Worsthorn of Stony Easton Lodge
June 10th, 12 midnight

Jane,

I know you were fond of C.

My heart is so full of grief as I write this that you must forgive me. I do not know if you were ever entirely convinced of C. being a Princess, but Jane, she is NOT. She is an impostor. A cobbler's daughter from Devonshire. A servant girl. You may have heard the news by now. I think all Bristol will be buzzing with it. I write because I cannot face anyone as yet. I feel so cast down, so – so – cheated.

C.'s real name is Mary Baker. She came to Bristol to look for work, then, finding none, decided to set sail for America. She did not have the fare (£5) so thought to beg for it, in the guise of a foreigner.

Dr Wilkinson's letters to the *Bath Herald* alerted C – (I must now call her Mary if I can. O Jane, this is such a distressing letter to write) – to the fact that she would soon be found out. This was the reason she ran away the first time, before the fever struck her down. She hoped to travel to Philadelphia on a ship which had already sailed. If she had vanished then, we would never have known what had happened to her, and never known who she really was.

Dr Wilkinson's letter in the newspaper was seen by Mrs Neale, Mary's former landlady in Bristol. She recognised the description of C. as being, in reality, none other than Mary Baker, who had dressed up one morning in odd clothes and set off to make her fortune, leaving her trunk behind. My heart beats fast at the shame of it. To be so taken in! But so were so many people! Shall I ever live it down? Jane, do come to me!

I must continue with my story, but sometimes I feel so overwhelmed.

Mrs Neale told me Mary had often behaved oddly, but never to this extent.

On Monday morning Mrs Neale called on Mr Mortimer and told him her suspicions. Mr Mortimer became convinced of the truth of her story, and came to me, to break the news as gently as he could.

Mr Mortimer arrived at Knole in the evening, closely followed by the son of a wheelwright, a handsome enough young man with an honest face. He told us he had met a girl answering to C.'s description on April 17th, before she entered Almondsbury, and though she would not talk to him she had happily drunk spirits, and he had thought her to be Spanish for she answered him with curious clicking noises of the tongue.

Mr Mortimer told me to expect C. to lie when faced with the truth, and our only hope was to frighten her by a confrontation with Mrs Neale. He said I must behave towards C. as usual, acting with the same affection and amusement. He was fearful she would run away again.

I called C. and requested her to dress in all her finery, for we were taking her to see Mr Bird in Bristol, to continue with her portrait. How the words choked me! She ran off gaily to dress herself, and I felt – I – who should not feel anything but horror at her duplicity – I felt that I was betraying her. I had become so fond of her.

When she reappeared she had on her turban with the blue feathers and jewelled clasp, and her wool dress with the gold embroidery, and she looked so charming that for an instant I believed the story to be false.

Will Frogley brought the carriage round and C. jumped in, salaaming to him very cheerfully and quite frightening Belmont, who is nervous of feathers but otherwise quite recovered in health. She chatted to me in her own language for most of the way, miming and laughing and waving to the people we passed, who stopped to stare, and one girl tossed a bunch of wild flowers into the carriage.

C. jumped up and cried (as she is wont to do) 'For me? For me? For me?' repeating the words many times to show off her command of the English language. For once I did not admire her cleverness, for at that moment I felt only pity, Jane, you may not understand this, but, yes, pity, for she enjoyed her role so much. I am convinced she would have made an excellent actress on the London stage. She is indeed wasted in her lowly position.

But I digress.

When the carriage stopped outside Mr Mortimer's lodgings and not at Mr Bird's, as C. expected, she looked enquiringly at me and her face became quite flushed. I believe she guessed at that moment that she had been found out. 'Me not picture?' she asked. 'No Caraboo,' I told her. 'There is a surprise for you inside.'

At that she looked relieved and pleased.

Many people had been running behind the carriage as we trotted into Bristol, and when we drew up at Mr Mortimer's quite a crowd collected.

Will Frogley used his whip freely to keep them from frightening Belmont, who does not like crowds.

C. bowed to them and salaamed, then leapt from the carriage with that elegance and grace which I can never admire too much. The crowd applauded, and she put out a hand to help me from the carriage, and made signs that I should salute the crowd also.

Mr Mortimer's housekeeper met us at the door and conducted C. to the kitchen, with strict instructions not take her eyes off C. for a second, for I was fearful she would guess our plot.

Mrs Neale awaited me in the parlour. An honest looking woman, and most respectful, in a clean print dress. She told me ALL. I think we sat for quite half and hour, and I wondered how C. was employed during that time. The housekeeper later informed me that they had been looking at books of China.

This letter is already so long that you will be yawning by now. I will not bore you with all the details of Mary's previous employments, Jane, not at the moment.

I asked Mrs Neale to wait in an adjoining chamber while I talked to Mary, and only to enter if I summoned her.

I sent for Mary and confronted her with damning proof of her real identity.

Jane, can you believe this? At first she made out SHE DID NOT UNDERSTAND ME. Falling on her knees she covered the hem of my dress with kisses, exclaiming 'Noddy! Moddy!' meaning Father and Mother in her 'own' language. Seeing this I became stern. 'Mary, get up, ' I told her, 'enough of this play acting. I KNOW you are an impostor and a liar, and have Mrs Neale, your landlady, here to prove it to both of us.'

At that she wept such tears! I felt as if my own heart would break, too, and after some time I raised her up and we clung together, both sobbing, her feathers becoming quite draggled and my pale blue silk dress quite spattered.

She begged me not to send for her father nor to cast her off. She told me that it was out of respect and love for me that she had been forced to carry on the deception. It had been impossible to break away, even though she wished it. She had never willingly cheated me in any way.

Jane, I believed her. She is scrupulously honest in all other ways. I promised not to send for her father, under certain conditions.

First, she must tell me all her past history, from the moment she was born. Secondly, we must have her real name, her parents' name, and where they lived.

She began at once a fanfaradiddle of a story of living four months in Bombay and on the Isle of France as nurse to a European family. Mr

Mortimer, who had entered the room by this time, soon proved the story false.

Mr Mortimer commanded Mary to be seated at the desk, and, giving her pen, ink and paper, he told her to write in full the past history of her life, saying he would not stir from the house until it was finished.

Mr Mortimer says that he thinks she will take several days. She is scribbling while he checks each page for faults and corrects the punctuation.

I myself proceeded back to Knole where I told the servants, who were very much affected. Mrs Pike has been in tears. Will Frogley said 'I cannot believe this, Ma'am, after all your goodness.' I could only press the poor fellow by the hand. I had not the heart to speak.

Affect.
Elizabeth

I forgot to say, Mrs Neale told me that on the morning C. left Knole (before her illness confined her to bed) she had visited Mrs Neale's lodgings, packed up her trunk, and paid her arrears of rent. It was after this that she had run to the quay and found the ship had sailed. On her return to Knole she dug up her clothes where she had left them in a field, and arrived at Knole, footsore and covered in mud. Can you wonder that she was sick? She had run across country, by the Duchess of Beaufort's wood, making her way through hedges and ditches, to avoid being seen.

Letter from Jane Worsthorn of Stony Easton Lodge to Mrs Worrall of Knole Park June 11th 1817

Dearest Elizabeth,

You must not blame yourself. We were all duped. I will come tomorrow. Where is she now?

Affect.
Jane

A thought has just struck me – unusual at so late an hour – did not Archbishop Whalley and Mr Coplestone send back a report on her writing saying it was a 'fine specimen of the Humbug language?' Now, Elizabeth, why did we not pay attention to *that*?

Dear Mrs Worrall,

I should have known! I, a man known for scientific discoveries. How blind I have been to be so readily taken in! I confess I had qualms when I came upon her in Bath, for when I first met her in the street she covered her face with her handkerchief and wept. Alas, I mistook the emotion for relief at seeing an old friend again. Now I see she feared she had been found out. When I addressed her as 'Princess Caraboo' she recovered at once, and proceeded to act as cleverly as before.

Can it be possible she should be deranged in her mind, and yet have been able to carry on her deception so long and with such consistency? We have heard of the power of maniacs to concert deep-laid plans with the greatest subtlety, but I recollect not *one* being carried out so successfully, for so long a time, and under such a variety of circumstances. I am at a loss to explain her consistency in play acting. Can she be so very clever? Can she be two characters at once? She has gulled half England. You, Madam, will always be remembered for your humane and charitable care of one you mistook for a friendless being from no known country. You have this to plead in excuse, should you be accused of gullibility.

They have printed broadsheets of verses about me in Bath. I trust, Madam, they will not come your way, to affront your ears.

> I remain, Madam,
> Your obedient, humble servant,
> C.H. Wilkinson

Letter from Jane Worsthorn of Stony Easton Lodge
to Mrs Worrall of Knole Park
June 16th 1817

Dearest E.

I do not wish to pain you but your name and that of Dr W. have become a byword in the county. I enclose clippings from various newspapers to show you the mischief that is being written. It is best to know the worst.

> Affect.
> Jane

I have picked out merely the relevant portions. The poems run for pages.

The following JEU D'ESPRITS *appeared in the different* BRISTOL *and* BATH NEWSPAPERS, *during the period which this imposture formed a topic of public conversation.*

CARABOO

OH ! aid me, ye spirits of wonder ! who soar
In realms of Romance where none ventur'd before ;
Ye Fairies ! who govern the fancies of men,
And sit on the point of Monk Lewis's pen ;
Ye mysterious Elves ! who for ever remain
With *Lusus naturæs*, and Ghosts of Cock-lane ;
Who ride upon broom-sticks, intent to deceive
All those who appear *pre-disposed* to believe,
And softly repeat from your home in the spheres
Incredible stories to *credulous* ears ;
With every thing marvellous, every thing new,
We'll trace a description of Miss CARABOO.

JOHANNA'S disciples, who piously came
To present babies' caps to their elderly dame,
Though all hope of their virgin's accouchement is o'er
They shall meet with the smile of derision no more ;
Their wonders were weak, *their* credulity small—
Caraboo was engendered by nothing at all !
And where did she come from ? and who can she be ?
Did she fall from the sky ? did she rise from the sea ?
A seraph of day, or a shadow of night ?
Did she spring upon earth in a stream of *gas-light* ?
Did she ride on the back of a fish, or sea-dog ?
A spirit of health, or a devil *incog.* ?
Was she wafted by winds over mountains and stream ?
Was she borne to our isle by the impulse of *steam* ?
Was she found in complete 'fascination' elate ?
Or discovered at first in chrysalis state ?
Did some philosophic analysis draw
Her component degrees from *some hot-water spa* ?
Did some chemical process occasion her birth ?
Did *galvanic* experiments bring her on earth ?
Is she new ? is she old ? is she false ? is she true ?
Come read me the riddle of Miss Caraboo.

Astronomers sage may exhibit her soon
As daughter-in-law to the man in the moon ;
Or declare that her visit accounts for the rain,
Which happened last year, and may happen again ;
That dark spots appear in the course she has run,
Coeval perhaps with the spots in the sun ;
That she *may* be connected with corsairs ; all these,
And as many more *possible things* as you please.

In what hand does she write ?—in what tongue does she speak ?
Is it Arabic, Persic, Egyptian, or Greek ?
She must be a *blue-stocking* lady indeed,
To write an epistle which no man can read ;
Though we have *some publishing scribes* I could name,
Whose *letters* will meet with a fate much the same.

She then wore no ear-rings, tho' still may be seen
The holes in her ears, where her ear-rings have been ;
Leather shoes on her feet ; a black shawl round her hair ;
And of black worsted stockings an elegant pair ;
Her gown was *black-stuff*, and my readers may guess,
If her *story* contains as much *stuff* as her *dress*.

Of the fam'd Indian Jugglers we all must have heard,
Who to gain a subsistence would swallow a sword ;
But men (without proof) who believe tales like these,
Will undoubtly *swallow* whatever you please.
I have heard, those who thought, that she wished to deceive,
After seeing her person have learned to believe ;
Even those, who have doubted the truth of her case,
Have forgotten their doubts when they look'd in her face.
I have never seen her ; but if when I see,
The truth of her tale is apparent to me,
I will cancel these lines, and most gladly rehearse
Her *swimming* and *fencing* in *beautiful* verse ;
In the graces and charms of my muse to adorn her,
Shall be the employment of Q in the corner.

The Bath Herald, June 10, 1817.

ODE TO MISS MOLLY BAKER *alias* PRINCESS CARABOO

O MOLLY, what a wag thou art—
So *effectually* to play the part
Of wandering, friendless Caraboo,
Bespeaks a talent few could boast
Ev'n from juggling India's coast—
But prythee, tell me—can it ALL *be true* ?

If thou, when heathen Greek inditing,
Didst rival RAPIER in his writing—
(So versatile thy nature,
And sweetly plastic every limb),
Like ROLAND *fence*, like *Dolphin swim*—
Thou art indeed an interesting creature.

Wert thou with ALL the men so shy,
As ev'n thy beauteous hand deny
In common salutation ?
Was there no *tender téte-a-téte*,
Thy *admirers* thus to fascinate,
Who puff'd thy beauty through the nation ?

Thy sloe-black eyes, and teeth so white,
(By Nature form'd to charm or bite)
With lady-airs in plenty—
Like opiates all the senses lull'd,
Of reason and of vision *gulled*,
Th'all-knowing *Cognoscenti.*

When to the *house-top* prone to stray,
And would'st to ALLA-TALLAH pray,
Had'st thou no HIGH PRIEST *near thee* ?
I mean not that imperious sun
Of reckless Juggernaut, but ONE
Well *pleas'd to assist* and hear thee ?

But where did'st learn (for Heav'n's sake),
To *swim* and *dive* like duck or drake,
When water-dogs pursue ?
And when for *pure* ablution quipp'd
Lurk'd there (as when Godiva stripp'd)
No *Peeping Tom*—or *wanton Makratoo* ?

Plague on that *meddling tell-tale* NEALE,
Eager thy *hist'ry to reveal,*
And *mar* the pleasing fable :—
Too sudden came the *denouement,*
Which proves thou art from *down-along,*
Where dumplings grace each table.

'Drat her *pug nose,* and *treacherous eyes,*
'*Deceitful wretch !*' the Doctor cries,
(No more inclin'd to flattery ;)
'When next I meet her (spite of groans)
'I'll rive her muscles, split her bones
'With my *Galvanic Battery.'*

But heed him not—for ('on my soul)
Whether at Bristol, Bath, or Knole,
I admir'd thy Caraboo.
Such *self-possession* at command,
The *bye-play* great—th'*illusion grand* :
In truth—*'twas every thing but* TRUE.

The Bristol Mercury

CRANIOLOGICAL DESCRIPTION OF CARABOO

ALTHOUGH many of our Readers think the system of Dr SPURZHEIM altogether fanciful, yet others continue of a different opinion. At all events, it may be curious to observe how far the organization of this girl's Head answers to these notions. We shall therefore record it,—not in mere jest, but as a matter of information.

Judging by this index, we should say, that she was constitutionally cold, and indifferent to physical love—or, to speak more intelligibly, not amorous. She has boundless AMBITION ; indeed this organ is so strongly marked, that to be thought a PRINCESS would be to her the *summum bonum.* She has great ATTACHMENT, or capability of firm friendship ; no quarrelsomeness, or wish to injure any one—which is, in the idiom of the science, no COMBATIVENESS, or DESTRUCTIVENESS. Not the least COVETIVENESS ; that is, she is perfectly indifferent to the acquirement or keeping of money or property. She has comparatively very little SECRETIVENESS : this organ is the one by which, the GALL-ites say, the possessor keeps his own secret,—wraps himself up in impenetrable mystery,—

keeping all real knowledge of himself and his intentions carefully concealed in his own heart, under a specious exterior. Now, how is it possible, that this organ, which it might be supposed CARABOO would have in the greatest perfection, should be defective, or how far her general conduct actually squares with it in point of fact, we leave to others to determine, contenting ourselves with recording the fact. The paradox will appear the wider when we state, that she has CIRCUMSPECTION or CAUTION in a *monstrous* degree. Her WARINESS is fully equalled by her VANITY. Her organization in this respect, if it could speak, would say plainly 'I, I, I, it is I, who can nose-lead you, and make fools of ye all ! I am this CARABOO, about whom you have made such a *fuss* ! It is I who have had one Lady offering upon her knees '*a bowl of cream for my Royal Highness !*'—it is I who have had another bowing in vacant amusement at the grandeur and sublimity of MY IMPERIAL MAJESTY !'

She has no BENEVOLENCE, but a great deal of VENERATION. The latter would induce her to behave kindly towards her Parents ; and the facts here bear the system out, for she has, from time to time sent them money, and written affectionate letters to them. As to her VENERATION in a religious point of view, it is a feeling of the heart which can only be known to herself.

It is doubtful whether she has IMAGINATION or IDEALITY—in other words, we cannot judge whether she could write a Novel or a Farce—although we venture to say that she herself forms an excellent SUBJECT for one.

She has INDIVIDUALITY—that is she remembers persons and things, and stores them up to be used as occasion requires. She is not wanting in FORM or COLOUR ; and has IMITATION in the greatest perfection.—She would soon rival Mr THELWALL or Mr MATTHEWS in *fac-similies* of every body whom she might choose to mimic.

In a word, if there be any truth in *Craniology*, she would, to the extent of her physical powers, make an admirable Actress ; but she would have nothing *original* : she would borrow here and there ; but she would never strike out any thing absolutely new. She has not much COMPARISON : so that probably her judgement of what is excellent and what is otherwise would not be correct. Hence she would be as apt to copy faults as perfections ; but the picture would be an exact copy—her *imitation* would be *the thing itself*. *

She has SPACE exceedingly developed—in other words, she must be of a roving disposition, and prefer liberty, and 'the whole world before her, where to chuse,' to good cheer and a collar, even although it were of gold—that is, she is fitted for a Gypsey—to which she will return, if there be faith in SPURZHEIM !— for we strongly suspect, that if the whole truth were known, she has been *three years* instead of three days amongst this ancient society of Vagabonds.

---

* After the discovery, she more than once expressed a wish, that the tale might be dramatized ; and nothing, she said, would have given her greater pleasure, than to have acted the part of CARABOO.

To sum up all, her *knowing faculties* infinitely outweigh her *animal propensities* ;—and if there should be any attempt to reclaim this stray sheep, her Guardian must take this for his guide— *if there be any truth in Craniology* !

The Bristol Mirror

THE
CONFESSION

AN OLD LADY BORN IN 1829

'Seven on us died, and I bein' the eldest can call to mind that I wasn't sorry, though Mother, who was a soft-hearted woman, 'ud cry a bit . . .

No, I didn't seem to hold with marryin' – saw too much of it. Saw me own sisters. There wasn't Parish nurses when I was young, nor chloroform. If the women died, they died. People took things as they come in those days, and if it hadn't been for some of the children dyin', how'd the poor ever have brought up a fam'ly?'

Mrs C. S. Poel, *A Hundred Wonderful Years*

CHAPTER ELEVEN

I Embark Upon the World

I was born, I think in 1791 or 1792, the third of eleven children. We kept no record of dates since my mother and father could not read or write. Seven of my brothers and sisters died in infancy. If my mother's next child was the same sex as the one she had lost, she used the same name again. That way she felt the deaths less keenly. Both Elizabeths died, and both Samuels. The third Susannah lived, and the second Thomas.

We needed few names.

I was the only Mary, and Henry the only Henry, for we both clung tenaciously to life.

My father is a cobbler in Witheridge in Devonshire. When I was a child we seemed prosperous enough, but after the Poor Laws came in and the Enclosures took place everyone in the village fell on hard times except the Squire. We could not keep a sheep on the common any more, nor our old horse. My father grew bitter. No one had money enough to buy the shoes he made, for the Squire bought *his* shoes in Exeter or London. Our old Vicar was too busy counting tithes to worry about a new pair of boots. He received tithes on every living thing, down to the eggs the hens laid, and spent his days counting each new thing in the village. On Sundays he denounced all those who had not paid their dues to the Church.

While Father could, he kept his horse and cart and took his shoes to Exeter to sell, but as the horse grew old and ill, he was unable to drive to market. My mother was always ailing from childbearing.

When I was young I helped the farmers in the fields, and at eight years old they set me to work spinning wool. I would drive the farmer's horses, or stand in the field with a clapper to scare the crows from the corn. I was as strong as a boy, though small, and would often be employed to weed the fields with the labourers.

I excelled at games. We played cricket in the evenings with a ball made from wood and sewn up inside a rabbit skin, or swam in the river, or shot with bow and arrow. Henry cut the arrow points so sharp I could kill a blackbird as easily with an arrow as a stone. I learnt to dive in the river and could catch a ball as good as any man. I was always of a wild disposition, more of a boy than a girl, and Mother despaired of me at times.

When I was sixteen I fell ill of the rheumatic fever. My mother thought I would die, as my sister Elizabeth had died the year before, at about my age. She dosed me with field herbs but I grew no better, so she called in the village wise woman, who had a face like a goat and smelt like one, too. She steamed millipedes in a pot over the fire and fed me the result, crushed to powder. I can still remember the taste. Before she left she tied a red thread round my wrist to ward off the evil eye, and a dead mouse round my throat, to help with the soreness.

My mother thought this witchcraft, and threw the dead mouse out of the window as soon as she left. The wise woman was standing below, peering into the pigsty to see how our sow was faring. She never visited us again.

After a long time the fever left me, though I felt very weak and my head hurt at times. I saw strange things and was sad one minute and happy the next, but my mother said that was natural for I had suffered much. I told myself stories as I lay on the pallet, but in so loud a voice my mother would hear through the floorboards and come up in a flurry, wanting to know which of my brothers or sisters had come home from work early. Mother always dressed in black, with a sackcloth apron, and her face was so white she would scare me when she appeared in the opening, for she looked so like death come to get me.

During my illness my parents must have discussed what to do with me should I recover. The cottage was cramped and I was just another mouth to feed and another body in a bed already full of children.

When I was able to walk again, and getting stronger, my mother told me I must go out to work in a situation where I would have my board and lodging. I was sixteen, and fully grown.

My mother asked around and found a satisfactory situation for me on the farm of a Mr Moon, at Bradford, near Witheridge.

I was to begin work immediately, as maid of all work and to help with the children.

How pleased I was! To escape from that crowded cottage, which stank of refuse and was so smoky from the fire, sleeping huddled with my brothers and sisters on the straw mattress, the sick with the well – listening to our parents bewailing the harshness of the times – it seemed like paradise.

I was anxious, too, to escape my father. In his bitterness he had grown short tempered and beat us when we disobeyed him. Since I was strong-willed I found it hard not to cross him.

If a soothsayer could have warned me of the adventures ahead, the

The entrance to Knole Park in Gloucestershire,
home of Elizabeth and Samuel Worrall

Kip's View of Knole Park c.1700

Princess Caraboo of Javasu, by Benjamin Barker *c.*1817 *Sabin Galleries*

hardships and terrors, I never would have left home with such high hopes. But OH! the excitement of it, if I had known what my adventures would bring!

My mother packed a few things for me in a small tin trunk. The carrier was bound for Bradford that day, and I was helped into the cart with strict warnings.

'Behave thyself sensibly, girl!'

'Do nowt that is giddy or wicked, Mary!'

'Work as hard as they bid thee, girl, and then a bit more!'

The smell of spring was already in the air, and off we set. Down the lane stood my brother Henry, waiting to say goodbye.

'Try not to cry, lass. I shall walk to Bradford, to visit thee soon.'

It began to rain.

My cloak gave me little protection from the weather, being much patched and darned. I huddled closer to the carter, for warmth. He seemed angry. He was a sour, thin man with a face like a turnip. It hid behind sprouting ginger hair and was covered in bumps as large as raspberries. He smiled not once on the journey – nor ever had, I expect, during the past fifty years.

I asked him (for I thought he might improve on acquaintance), 'Will I like Mrs Moon? Will she make me work very hard?'

He chewed a little, as though he had found the remains of yesterday's dinner between his black gapped teeth, and said, 'Couldn't say.'

Would he mind my snuggling close to him? I shyly asked, for it was now raining hard, and I was chilled.

He ruminated some more, shrugged his shoulders, whipped up the horse, scratched his head with such violence that I thought he would lose his hat, and replied, 'Couldn't say.'

I pursued the question of the Moons.

'Do they have many children? A large farm, horses, cows, and suchlike?'

At that he became silent, as though struck deaf. He then shouted at his horse for going so slow, and whipped it so savagely that the poor beast tried to break into a gallop. The nearside wheel hit a stone and the cart tilted wildly. I was thrown on top of the carrier, while my trunk bounced and rattled in the back of the cart like a dried up pea in a pod.

When we righted ourselves the carrier shouted at me, accusing me of trying to compromise him. He had few kind words for women it seemed, and none for me. To show him how offended I was I moved to the other end of the bench, wrapped my cloak round me, and hid my face in my bonnet – letting him know how deeply he had upset me.

I felt miserable, utterly alone, with no desire to work for Mrs Moon. I hated her very name! Mrs Moon? Why not Mrs Sun?

I thought of Henry. How I would miss him! My mother, too. But Henry had always petted me, and stood up for me, while my mother urged me to stop fantasising and daydreaming.

'Work Hard, girl!' she would say to me. But I wanted life. I wanted adventure. I did not want to work on a farm.

At last we halted in front of a long, low, stone farmhouse. It had curiously twisted chimneys, and two trees at either end like soldiers standing guard. The yard was knee deep in mud and full of cows come in for milking. Hens pecked round their feet and a gross of pigs rootled in the dung-heap.

Standing in the middle of it all, on pattens three inches high, her dress covered by a sacking apron, and another piece of sacking thrown over her head to protect her hair from the rain, stood Mrs Moon. She was round, red-faced and cheerful, the little I could see of her, and her eyes lit up when she saw me. She came towards the cart, brandishing a milking pail in one hand and a stool in the other, crying, 'You'm arrived in time to begin milking!' She said she hoped we would get on together, for the last maid-of-all-work had been a 'niminy piminy thing' and frightened of the children.

'Such a tiny creature you are!' she added, as I climbed down from the cart and she looked me up and down. She wasn't expecting someone so small and thin, and she hoped I would not prove a weakling, for she had no time to nurse me.

I assured her I was tough, and tried to look it, but I was shaking from cold and nervousness. She called a labourer to haul down my trunk from the cart, which he did as though it had been filled with feathers. I said goodbye to the carter, who looked relieved to be rid of me, and Mrs Moon and I went into the house. She lent me a dry cloak and a pair of pattens, then took me to the milking shed, where the cows were waiting.

Here I met the children. Seven of them, so ragged and dirty you could not tell who was a boy and who a girl. Seated in rows, down to the youngest of nearly six years, they were milking the cows. The eldest girl, whose name I later found out was Hannah, was my age. She was singing to her cow, in a sweet, high voice, her head pressed against the brown flank.

Mrs Moon was very particular about the milking. I had often milked cows on the farm at Witheridge, and never been told off, but with Mrs Moon it was, 'Sure you milked the udders dry?' And she would come and see for herself. Or, 'Make sure you wash them properly with warm water before you start – are your hands clean?'

The only clean part of the children was their hands. We only had one piece of apparel each, and when that was washed we sat round the stove in the kitchen, steaming, having bathed at the same time. We waited, huddled in blankets, until our clothes were dry.

I worked hard, and so did the children. Being teased about being so small and thin I often used to carry a sack of corn or apples on my back, pretending it was light, endeavouring to do more than the labouring men, and so be rewarded by praise from Mrs Moon.

Often I got so tired I fell asleep at the evening milking. The cow would become restless when my hands stopped, and she would turn and look at me sternly, blowing her hot milky breath in my face and kicking over the bucket if I did not notice her. Then Hannah would stop singing and come and wake me.

Once Henry came to see me. The children were so excited by a strange man visiting the farm that they hung onto him and would not attend to their duties. Seeing him, so dear and friendly, with his tangle of brown curls and his grey eyes looking anxiously to see if I was well and happy, I began to cry. Big tears rolled down my cheeks and fell plop! on the ground, and Mrs Moon came out to see why work had stopped and the cows had not been milked and she was very angry.

It upset me to see him, for he reminded me of home and the happy times we had had. On the Moon's farm I was always tired. I rose at dawn and when it grew dark and I was able to slip away to bed, I was too tired to do more than curl up and sleep. I did not notice the sun shining, except when it was hot in the dairy, and two summers went by without my noticing.

Henry visited me only twice.

I never had time to talk to him. It was a long journey for him and he knew his visits made me unhappy, so he decided not to come any more. I was working too hard to care.

Mrs Moon often told me she was pleased with my work, and after two years on the farm I decided to ask for a rise, so that I could send more of my wages to my mother. We were in the kitchen, and I was preparing the supper.

I had begun to peel the potatoes and Mrs Moon was chopping turnips.

I asked her, 'Missus, could I have more a week for my work? A shilling instead of tenpence? It's only twopence a week more. I've been here along of two years.'

I kept my eyes fixed on the table. It was difficult to ask for more money, but I was determined.

The knife in Mrs Moon's hands cut faster and faster through the turnips. Turnip peelings were flying about the kitchen as though bewitched.

I looked up.

Mrs Moon's face was flushed an angry red. For the first time, she was furious with me. She banged on the table with her fist, making the potatoes jump and roll off.

'I'm *astonished* at you, Mary!' she shouted. Hadn't they always liked me? Hadn't they treated me as one of their family?

'When we've been so fond of you. When we feed you so well,' she added, with a cold look, accusing me of gluttony. I had *nothing* to complain about. I was a venomous viper she had foolishly nourished – to ask for MORE when I already had so MUCH!

I had a bed, with a flock mattress, and only two of the children to share it with. 'How many girls of your class get luxury like that?' She lamented that they had spoiled me, not worked me hard enough, given me time to think!

'And how do you reward us, Mary? Eh? With sheer ingratitude, discontent, and heathen greed!'

Too ashamed to reply, I hung my head.

She relented a little. I was greedy for money, she said, because I was too young to know better. However, if I really felt so restless I had better pursue my fortune elsewhere. Then she patted me on the head and told me she would miss me, and so would the children, for they loved my stories.

So I left.

Hannah cried when she said goodbye, and I cried, too. Mrs Moon wrote me a good recommendation. I felt that I deserved it, but refrained from saying so.

I packed my trunk and asked Mrs Moon to give it to the carrier when next he came by, and my father would pay for the delivery with my wages.

I wrapped myself in my cloak, adjusted my bonnet, picked up my bundle of necessaries, and started my long walk home.

WARNING TO THIEVISH SERVANTS

'Any clerk, apprentice, or servant whatsoever, feloniously stealing any goods, chattels, money, bond, bank note, check upon Banker's Draft, Promissory note, Bill of Exchange, or other valuable security or effects, from his master or employers. Penalty: Transportation for fourteen years, or imprisonment only, or kept to hard labour in the Gaol or House of Correction or Penitentiary House (not exceeding) three years.'

W. M. Robinson, *Magistrates Pocket Book* (1825)

CHAPTER TWELVE

I Become a Cook

My father was sitting on a bench outside the house when I arrived. He was patching up a pair of the vicar's boots.

He said it was kind of Mrs Moon to give me a day off to visit them. She must value my services.

When I told him I had left the farm because Mrs Moon would not raise my wages to a shilling a week he began to shout at me. 'You'm bigoted and ungrateful, Mary! You'm a disgrace! You'm no daughter of mine!'

My mother came out. She had been crying, for my baby sister had just died. My father was short of work and there was little food in the house. The house felt terrible sad.

I stayed home only a few days, to help them. Then I decided to walk to Exeter to see if I could find myself a new situation. I did not know how to obtain employment, so sitting by the roadside I began to cry.

A stout fisherwoman with a red kindly face asked me why I was bawling so. I replied that I wanted employment.

She directed me to Mr Brooke's place, a shoemakers, in Fore Street.

Because I was a country girl, Mrs Brooke liked my appearance very much, but she was afraid that I was an apprentice that had run away from her mistress. She offered me £8 a year, if I returned to my father's for a fortnight while she enquired if I was a runaway apprentice or not.

At the end of the two weeks, Mrs Brooke hired me. I was expected to wash, iron and cook, to which I was not accustomed. My duties included scrubbing and polishing the floors in the house and the steps outside the front door, as well as cutting the firewood and making up the fires. Filling the baths and emptying the slop pails hurt my back; it was even harder work than the farm. I slept in a back room off the kitchen. It was filled with black beetles which crawled up the wall beside my pallet on the floor, and fell on my face in the night.

From the barred window in the kitchen I could look up to see the feet of passers by. One day a carter came into the basement and asked me if I had any food to sell. I was tempted. He said I could keep the money to buy pretty things. 'Say the dog has eaten it,' he told me.

I said the Brookes kept no dog and he laughed at me.

My mother had warned me that honesty was very important. Once you started to thieve you could not stop and ended up transported or hanged. A brother of hers had been hanged for stealing a loaf of bread. I did not want to be a thief, so I said no. The carter was disappointed. Some cooks, he told me, sold him whole legs of mutton and did so well out of the business they were able to leave service.

I cried when he had gone, but I was glad I had said no.

I stayed with Mrs Brooke two months. I was unable to work with the kitchen range. It set out deliberately to spite me, belching smoke all over the kitchen. I would kick it and cry MONSTER! and BRUTE! but it never worked.

When I told Mrs Brooke I had to leave because the kitchen range smoked so, she was cross but was sorry to see me go. She told me she wished me well. I had been an honest servant, and a willing one.

She paid me £2 to thank me for my work.

I had never had so much money. I felt rich, young, and the sun was shining.

There was a street market in Exeter that day. Barrows piled high with fish, oysters and eels, crabs and lobsters with claws tied together and vicious eyes, cocks and hens squawking. The noise was deafening and excited me.

In the middle of the street stood a hare, dancing on his hind feet and banging a kettledrum with his paws. A crowd of men surrounded him. His owner, a fat Frenchman with a straggling moustache, came round to collect money, and I gave him a penny.

A pig called Toby with glasses on his nose and a ruff round his neck, wearing a small black hat, was counting numbers. His master drew the numbers in the dust and told Toby to point to the right number with his snout. This he did so comically, with such grunts and efforts at learning, peering through his glasses at the dust, that I laughed so much I gave his master a penny, too.

But *still* I had money!

There was a barrow selling clothes. They hung from the top, spilled over the sides, and lay piled on the ground around it – velvet waistcoats, breeches with gold lacings, a cutaway coat of blue with daisies embroidered all over it, but a hole where a sword had cut the cloth; a coachman's coat, greasy and stained, with metal buttons the size of soup plates. Had he died, to give his greatcoat for sale?

And then, the women's clothes!

Oh how I envied the ladies who wore such garments!

There was a white wool shawl of such softness it seemed to float. Dresses of all colours and materials hung from the barrow. White muslin sprigged with flowers, cotton dresses, silks, spotted, plain, paisley patterned. Here one with foodstuff spilt all over, there another with wine down the front. Flame and red and purples and orange. White, always white, so luxurious, so wonderful! I had only had two dresses since I was a child. Patched and darned, they went up and down in the family until they were too worn out to be used any more, and then they were cut up for bindings for the new babies.

There were cloaks, too. Cloaks with fur collars and cloaks with velvet trimmings, bonnets of straw and bonnets festooned with ribbons and flowers, a black bonnet with a sweeping ostrich feather, a clutch of bonnets with laced edgings; boots and shoes and walking sticks, satin slippers and parasols! Oh it was wonderful! I was so excited I began to grab at things to try on.

I put on a bonnet and measured my feet against a pair of satin slippers, I placed a shawl over my shoulders. I held up a silk dress and danced with it in my arms.

I spent all the money I had.

Clutching my new clothes in my arms I ran from the market place. When I came to a hedge I changed, my hands so clumsy with excitement I could scarce button the dress, which fitted perfectly.

It was white muslin. It flowed round my legs like water. The bonnet sat snugly on my head, and if I looked from the corners of my eye I could see the lace trimming. The satin slippers were made for dancing. I knew what it felt like to be a lady. I pulled my shawl round my shoulders for warmth, and to hide the scorch mark on the bodice.

I imagined the admiration of my parents and the envy of my friends. My head was full of fantasy. I was a young lady come to visit, not a daughter.

I did not notice my father's face grow red when he saw me. He was very angry. Words rose and choked him. He spluttered and looked ready to die from fear. 'You'm a thief!' He shouted at me. He rose, and came forward as though to strike me. 'You'm been stealing from your mistress!' I said that was untrue, it was a lie, I had come by my clothes honestly, they were my wages for the months I had worked.

'You'm a harlot,' he shouted. 'You'm been nothing but trouble since you'm been born. You'm bigoted, you'm MAD, never content, always wanting more, more and more – and now this!'

The noise of his shouting brought my mother.

'Your clo's, Mary,' she cried, 'you'm not to wear that dress! It be for a lady! You be disgracing us, girl, take 'un off, Mary, take 'un off. Oh Mary, whatever have you done girl? What will people say of us?'

'Harlot,' said my father. He hit me hard, once, twice. I ducked away, but my mother followed me, clutching at my arm. 'Please Mary, hard tho' your heart be, strong willed as you are, listen to us Mary, it's wicked you are to ape your betters, girl.'

But I wouldn't part with my dress.

I stayed home only six days, during which time no-one spoke to me. I met Mr and Mrs Moon on market day selling calves. They would not speak to me either. They saw my new dress and said I must have procured my clothes dishonestly as they looked too good. Knowing my innocence, I was upset. I cried.

I left home, wandering through different parts of the country, not knowing where to go. I left my dress at my father's, and had no money in my pocket so I went begging at different houses. Some people gave me money, saying it was a pity for such a young creature to wander about the country, others proposed taking me up as a vagabond and horse-whipping me, which made me cry very much.

One evening I began to think of taking my own life.

I had no friends in the world, and no money.

I stood on the street corner, crying.

Unable to bear it I went down a lane and took my apron strings and tied them together. I fastened them round the branch of a tree and from there intended to fasten them round my neck.

Shutting my eyes I prayed, 'Oh Lord be with me in my last hour that has now come.'

I was about to tighten the noose when a voice inside my head said – I heard it distinctly – 'Cursed are they that do murder, and sin against the Lord.'

So I untied the string. Being unhappy I was crying a great deal as I walked, and at length I met an elderly gentleman in blue breeches and buff greatcoat who said, 'My pretty girl, what is the matter with you, crying so? Where are you going?'

I told him my story, and the particulars of my being about to hang myself. He was much agitated, and reasoned with me strongly about the wickedness of it, and gave me five shillings, saying, 'Go away in Peace. Put your trust in the Lord, and He will never forsake you.'

OBSERVATIONS ON JAIL AND HOSPITAL FEVER

'There are but few of the sick . . . that find their way into the great hospitals of London, which probably is to be imputed to there being but one day a week allotted for the admission of patients. Before a recommendation can be procured and the stated day come round, the sick person is either better or so much worse that he cannot be moved; or is perhaps dead.'

Dr J. Hunter, *Medical transactions of the College of Physicians* (1779)

CHAPTER THIRTEEN

I Fall Sick

With the five shillings in my pocket I felt happier and decided to walk to Taunton.

I arrived just as dusk was falling and began to look for lodgings. I found a bed at the 'Three Queens' in a dormitory packed with mattresses. It did not look to be too filthy. The price of sharing a double bed with flock mattress was 2½d and a feather bed to myself was 4d. I took the shared bed to make my money last.

The lodging house was clean and I stayed there three days while I looked round Taunton for work. There was none to be had. I despaired after the three days was up and set off to walk from Taunton to Bristol, a distance of 75 miles. My landlady told me Bristol was a fine town and there were opportunities there.

I had spent all my money. I begged my way from Taunton to Bristol, knocking on doors and asking for food. If I got money I slept in lodgings, if not, I climbed into a hayloft or slept between hayricks on the ground.

I saw very few people, but I was frightened, for I was young and unprotected and the law recommended that vagrants should be sent home or delivered to the workhouse. If I was picked up as a vagrant I would be sent back to my father who would beat me for having no employment. There was no room for me at home, and I liked the freedom of wandering.

The threat of the workhouse *did* worry me. My mother told me that once inside they never let you go. You were starved, and worked to death, and any possessions you had were taken from you. You were put in the stocks or locked in the cellar for any offence against the rules, from grumbling at the food to complaining about the rats. My mother said workhouses were always in old houses, and full of rats. She said she would die rather than be sent to one.

When I reached Bristol I was very hungry. When I asked for food I was directed to Mr Freeman, of the Stranger's Friend Society, who lived by the drawbridge. I thought with a name like 'stranger's friend' Mr Freeman must be a good man.

I knocked on the door, which was opened by a servant girl. I explained that I was in want of charity. I had no money and had eaten nothing for some time. She called her master.

Mr Freeman, when he appeared, looked benevolent. He had bushy white eyebrows and snuff down his smoking jacket. His head was a polished egg shape with wisps of white wool over his ears and a sprinkling of hairs on his chin.

He looked hard at me with his round blue eyes and I blushed, thinking he must be seeing all the wickedness in my head.

He began to ask me questions. My father's name? Being unable to think of a suitable one, I answered, 'My father died when I was two, sir.'

'H'm,' he said, as though he disbelieved me.

'And your mother?'

I began to stammer, getting flustered.

'My m–m–mother died as well, sir, at the s–same time, sir.'

'Of what did they die?'

'O! . . . of the . . . pox, sir.'

'Did they have spots, or fever, or both?'

'Both, sir, terrible bad they were, sir, my small brother and my two brothers died as well, sir.'

'Who brought you up then, if everyone around you died?'

'O! . . . M–my Aunt, sir, but she's dead too, now, sir.'

'My poor girl.' Mr Freeman did not appear to mean this. His tongue clicked against his teeth with tch . . . tch . . . tch . . . noises.

He took a pinch of snuff, looked at his watch, sniffed, could not make up his mind what to do, and said, 'Come again in the morning, girl, and I will discover more about your parents.'

As I had told him they were both dead, and all my relatives as well, this sounded bad. I resolved never to go near the house again.

On parting Mr Freeman became kind. He handed me 4/- for lodgings and food, so that I was able to set off next morning on the London road out of Bristol, intending to walk to London to try my fortune there.

To my great distress the 4/- was stolen from me shortly after I left Bristol, so I was penniless again. In Calne I decided to beg for food. I knocked on the back door of a prosperous looking house, set back from the road with a painted white gate.

It looked as though they would have food to spare and I did not see any guard dogs. A stout, red-faced cook answered my knock. 'Be off!' she cried as soon as she set eyes on me, 'we don't give nothin' to beggars!' 'O please,' I begged, 'I'm so hungry,' and I looked pleadingly at her, to coax her into kindness. 'Go 'way,' she said, backing into the house, 'go back where you came from. I'd be ashamed, at your age, to go beggin' from respectable houses!' She made as if to slam the door. 'Martha,' called a voice, 'what is it, Martha?'

The man who appeared had a pinched, gaunt face. When I saw him I knew something bad was about to happen. My knees shook, and I went cold.

'Come in,' he said and stood aside, to let me enter.

I shook my head. 'No, no, sir, it's all right, sir, I have work, really I do. Sir, it's all a mistake.' He caught hold of my arm. 'O please sir, I must go now, sir,' I begged. I struggled, but he was strong. He pushed me into the house and down a narrow passageway to a study lined with books. A black cat was curled up in the only chair. There was a smell of beeswax and damp. It was a dark, cold room.

'Your name?' he asked, standing with his back to the fire, which smoked. He had a sharp way of speaking, as though daring me to lie. He took obvious pleasure in my discomfort.

'Mary, sir.'

'How old are you, Mary?'

'Sixteen, sir.'

'How come you to be begging, Mary?'

'I am hungry, sir, and have no shelter for the night.'

'I thought you said you had work, Mary?'

'O yes, sir, yes, I have work.'

'Where, Mary?'

'In Exeter, sir.'

'But you are not in Exeter, now, Mary. Perhaps you have left your work? Perhaps you are an apprentice, run away? What was your work, Mary?'

'No! No sir, not run away! A cook, sir, if it please you, sir.'

'Is that so, Mary. And why, if I might ask, did you leave?'

'The fire smoked so, sir, and I didn't like the black beetles.'

'I see, Mary. Perhaps you are a trifle fussy, eh? Perhaps you think yourself too good for hard work? Perhaps your mistress turned you out? Perhaps you are a thief?'

'No, O no, I never stole, O sir, I promise I wouldn't steal! I became ill, sir, and had to leave.'

'Ill, eh? Hard work made you ill? Did you not run away, Mary, leaving behind you a job you did not like, and a mistress who was not to your liking?'

'No, no, really, no sir, I did not. I was hired, sir, and then I gave in my notice after three months, and left.'

'Where is your family, Mary?'

'I have no family, sir.'

'O? No father or mother, Mary? No sisters or brothers? Perhaps there is a relative still living?'

'No sir.'

'All dead of the plague I suppose, Mary. Come, come you need a better story than that.'

'Yes sir.'

He was silent, then asked me how I came to be in Calne. I told him I had walked from Bristol.

'Mary is not a very long name, is it, Mary? What is your surname?'

I could not think of any name, but catching sight of a loaf of bread upon the table, 'Mary Baker, sir,' I told him.

He did not seem convinced. 'I am a Constable of this Parish,' he told me. 'Of which fact you were unaware when you knocked so boldly on my door, begging. I do not believe you are speaking the truth. Tomorrow I will take you to the Justice of the Peace to be sworn to the Parish, then you will be returned to your family, or sent to the penitentiary. Until then, I will lock you in this room.'

A dog began howling, and the man's face twisted with rage. 'More beggars, I dare swear,' he muttered. 'I shall be gone a moment, to see what the noise is about. Do not move. I will be back directly.'

The door banged. I heard the click of the key in the lock. When the noise of his footsteps died I ran to the window. It was high in the wall, and narrow, but I thought I could squeeze through if I could reach it.

I dragged a table underneath the window and scrambled onto the sill. For one terrifying moment I thought I would stick. Desperation gave me strength. Scraping myself raw on the window frame I scrambled through the opening and landed in a heap on the grass below.

Once safely on the ground, I fled.

I remember laughing so much with relief at my escape that I became quite ill with it. After that I felt so tired that my feet seemed made of lead. Within thirty miles of London I was violently sick; the road heaved up and down in front of me, and I wanted to die.

I must have fainted, for the next thing I knew I was being lifted up by a waggoner. I was frightened, for I did not know where I was. He called out, 'Look! She's alive! I told you she was not dead!'

His passengers, two ladies in red cloaks bound for London, exclaimed nervously that perhaps he should not hold me, for I might have the plague, or, at the least, an infectious fever. I tried to tell them that I had eaten bad food somewhere, and was over-fatigued, but the words would not come.

Since I could not stand, the waggoner offered to take me to London if I was bound that far. I told him, weakly, that I had no money. He said he did not mind. He added he would not like to leave a girl my age in such a condition, under a hedge, for I would surely die if he abandoned me there. 'I have seven children at home,' he told me, 'and I don't know to what end they'll come.' Then he lifted me up into the back of the waggon, under the canvas, and tucked me up among the trusses of woollen drapery. The two ladies turned to offer me bread and cheese, but I could not eat. The waggon was close, and smelt of horse and wool and grease.

While I lay there, half asleep, I heard the voice of the waggoner, walking beside the waggon, flicking his whip, and the soft 'ohs' and 'ahs' of the ladies listening to him, with the occasional scream if the tale was alarming.

He was telling them stories of things that had happened to waggoners of his acquaintance. I lay there, half listening, and it seemed to me that the things were happening at that moment, and several times I woke in a sweat of fear.

He informed the ladies that a friend of his had drunk too much gin and water and fallen asleep on the shafts of his waggon and fallen off and been crushed to death. This, he added, was a fate common to many waggoners, for most of them drank too much. For this reason, he added, his breath coming in puffs of hot rum, he allowed nothing but water to pass his lips. Even in my semi-conscious state I was forced to smile.

In a lively fashion he proceeded to describe another friend, for whom furious driving had become a habit. This man drove at six or seven miles an hour down the middle of the road, forcing other vehicles into the ditch. A second friend had taken a waggon loaded with gunpowder to the village of Talk on the Hill, Staffordshire, when the friction of the axle tree set fire to the gunpowder, and the explosion had blown him skywards and scattered limbs for miles. A house had fallen upon its inhabitants, bruising them in a shocking manner – and leaving the village little more than a heap of ruins.

The ladies now hanging on his every word, he told them of an armed robbery which had happened to a friend of a friend, who had been held up by a man dressed in a white dress, or smock. When the robber thrust his pistol into the waggoner's face, it had only flashed in the pan, so that he was simply scorched. He had been able to kill his assailant with a horse pistol in the ensuing struggle.

The tinkling of the horses' harness, the smacking of the waggoner's whip as he walked, and the jolting and bumping of the broad wheels of the waggon must have finally lulled me to sleep, for the last thing I remember was that the waggoner had left his waggon unattended outside an inn in Bristol, and been robbed of a truss of drapery goods, half a firkin of butter, and a box of confectionery.

After that I remember nothing.

When we reached Hyde Park Corner the waggoner told us to get down, for he could take us no further.

I found it difficult to stand.

The women were kind. They seemed concerned about me and helped me down from the waggon. They asked me where I was going. I told them I knew no one and had nowhere to go, so, supporting me on either side, they helped me to the door of St George's Hospital, where they sat me down on the step. The doors were locked and no one answered when they rang the bell, so they left me.

I remained there about a quarter of an hour, when the watchmen came and found me. They asked me who I was, and took me to the watch-house. I could not reply through illness and fatigue.

The watchmen left me and returned with Mr Burgess, a Physician of the hospital. He shook his head and said that I was in a very dangerous state.

He helped me into the hall and settled me in front of a blazing fire. The fire reminded me of Hell and the Devil and I clung to Mr Burgess. I was so hot and feverish I did not know what I was doing. I babbled that the Devil would get me, I was wicked, I had been vain and thoughtless. Mr Burgess repeated again and again, 'God is Merciful. God has pity on sinners,' while I sobbed.

Then he left to see if there was room for me in one of the wards. He woke one of the walking patients and asked her to come and help him look after me. Together they undressed me and put me to bed. Here I stayed a month, ill of brain fever.

My head was shaved and blistered to ease the fever and my back cupped at the same time. Brown paper was used to spread the blisters. It was very painful and I used to cry out when I saw the doctor coming. Mr Burgess told me without blistering and cupping I would never recover my health. As for dying, did I not remember my fear of Hell fire?

During my illness the nurses told me whenever I recovered consciousness I would ask them if I was dead yet.

When I felt stronger I asked Mr Burgess to let me go downstairs to the yard to get some air. The smell in the hospital was very bad, though the floors were swept, scrubbed and sanded each day. Mr Burgess told me that I was not strong enough, I was weaker than I thought.

I persisted, and, seeing me so determined, Mr Burgess said if I would carry the tea-kettle that was on the fire to the end of the ward, he would let me go down into the yard.

I picked up the kettle, not knowing that the water was already boiling. The handle was very hot and I could not hold it. I slipped on the sanded floor and would have fallen if Mr Burgess had not caught me. I scalded myself very badly, and Mr Burgess barely escaped being scalded himself.

After this I was kept to my bed a whole month, and when I got better I was moved from the Fever ward to the Decline ward, where I stayed until I had strength to leave the hospital.

The more that I saw people die around me, the more determined I became to survive.

When Mr Burgess pronounced me fully recovered, a difficulty presented itself. Where should I go?

The matron and nurse asked me where I had been going – which was nowhere – and whom I knew – which was no one, and they spoke to the clergyman of the Hospital, Mr Puttenden, and he recommended me to some ladies who got me a place at Mrs Mathew's; No. 1 Clapham Road-Place.

The next afternoon, with Mr Puttenden accompanying me and a guinea in my pocket which Mr Burgess had kindly give me, I walked to No. 1 Clapham Road-Place, where Mrs Mathews awaited me.

ADVICE TO FEMALE SERVANTS

'Be very careful of your reputation for virtue and discretion in regard of the other sex; for it is the foundation of your happiness in this world; and the loss of it will bring you to misery. Avoid as much as possible going out in the *evening*, especially on frivolous errands. Be cautious as to whom you give your company. "EVIL COMMUNICATIONS CORRUPT GOOD MANNERS." Never go to *fairs*, *dances*, nor to *theatres*. Ask yourself, before you engage in any pleasuring scheme – what may be the end of it? . . . '

W. Kitchiner, *The Complete Servant* (1827)

CHAPTER FOURTEEN

The Jew's Wedding

Mrs Mathews' creaking leather stays made her a demanding mistress. She dressed in black, with gold-rimmed spectacles on a chain round her neck, and her grey hair pulled back so tightly not a curl marred the severity of her appearance. Her daughter, Miss Betsey, was fourteen years old. There was no sign of Mr Mathews. I often wondered how he had dared beget Miss Betsey.

Mrs Mathews employed me to please Mr Puttenden, of whom she was very fond. She was a woman of strict principles, one of them being that no man must be allowed to cross the doorstep – except Mr Puttenden, who, being a clergyman, was exempt. She would not allow me to go out of the house alone, not even to take a message; nor could I have an afternoon off, unless there was some urgent reason of which she approved.

Miss Betsey and I went to church, walking behind Mrs Mathews, myself two paces behind Miss Betsey, and both of us wearing deep bonnets so that only the very tips of our noses showed. My bonnet was dark straw, untrimmed, suitable for a servant of some eighty years or more. I wore a grey stuff cloak, and we walked as though in funeral procession. We did not walk fast, for this could be seen as frivolity, nor look up, for that might be provocation. Mrs Mathews herself walked with determination. Lingering in the sunshine was a wanton pleasure.

At the beginning of my employment, Mrs Mathews was so strict that I pined for my freedom. I know she had it in mind to lock me in the attic bedroom should she need to leave the house suddenly – Miss Betsey told me – but the need never arose. In the first year I stayed with her, Mrs Mathews almost never went out, except to church, and after the first year I believe she was fond of me, and trusted me not to go outside the house on my own, nor to encourage men.

My routine was always the same. I was out of bed by five and lit the kitchen stove, putting the kettle on to boil. After I had cleaned the kitchen,

I laid the fires and heated more water for washing. When I took the water upstairs I woke Mrs Mathews and Miss Betsey, and drew the curtains in their room, then went downstairs to lay the table for breakfast, and to dust, sweep and polish until I heard Mrs Mathews descend the stairs with a swish of her black silk dress.

She would march past me into the kitchen. I would stop whatever I was doing and follow her, wiping my hands on my apron. Taking a key she would unlock the larder door.

She would then hand me a loaf of bread. 'Thank you, Ma'am,' I had to say, and bob a curtsey – three eggs – ' thank you, Ma'am,' and a pat of butter and some dripping. 'Thank you, Ma'am'.

She counted every slice of bread and every scrape of dripping. I was proud of my hands and rubbed them with grease whenever I could to stop them cracking and becoming red, and she would be puzzled by the amount of dripping that vanished every night. 'The mice, Ma'am.'

We fed extremely well. I cooked the meals, and ate the same food as Mrs Mathews and Miss Betsey, so that I became quite plump and worried about fitting into my dresses, of which I had but two.

Mrs Mathews was greedy over food. I began to look forward to meals as the only pleasure to be had. The days were so dull. Always the same. The hands of the clock moved slowly round – Spring, Summer, Autumn, Winter – and I did not know what the seasons were, nor whether it was cold or hot, wet or dry.

Mrs Mathews found me a good servant and obedient. Liking me, she wished to improve my mind. She taught me to read and gave me religious tracts to practise on, and permitted me to use the books in her bookcase, which were books of sermons.

Miss Betsey was kind. When she came home from school she would sit at the kitchen table and tell me to place myself opposite her. When we were settled she would write the alphabet and words for me to copy. I was so excited at learning to read and write that I worked well into the night, straining my eyes with the guttering candle, trying to see the words I had made. In this way I learnt very fast and spent my leisure time reading the tracts and sermons Mrs Mathews brought home to improve my mind.

Mr Puttenden was pleased with the results of my schooling. He came to talk to me and ask me to read the tracts aloud to him so that we could discuss what they said. He was a short, stout man with a rolling way of walking, as though he had been a seaman at one time. His teeth were blackened from chewing his pipe. I was fond of him. His anger could be terrible, but only because it was so shocking, for he was a real gentleman and very kind. He had seen some dreadful things in his life, he said, but his belief in the goodness of human nature never faltered.

He would come into the kitchen when I was working and one day he leant upon the table and addressed me thus; 'Mary, as a friend and one who has your best interests at heart, it grieves me to hear you when you say your parents are dead. I would like to help you, but how can I be of help when you say you have no relations, no friends, no one who cares whether you live or die? Mary, Mary, consider! If you have parents, think how happy they would be if they are told of your present situation! Think how pleased they would be to hear how fond we are of you! Think how delighted and proud they would be to hear that you are learning to read and write. Think of their sufferings, if they do not know where you are or what has become of you! Think of your mother's tears, your father's distress, if they think you ill, or dead!'

This upset me very much and set me thinking. I heard myself telling Mr Puttenden that my parents were alive and lived in Devonshire. I gave him their address, too, and told him about my brothers and sisters, and how much I missed Henry. It was such a relief to be able to talk about them. I could not stop, once I started.

Mr Puttenden was very kind. As soon as he found out where my parents lived he sent a messenger to Witheridge to ask about them. He discovered that my mother was still ailing and worried about me, and my father, though well, was suffering from lack of business.

After this Mr Puttenden wrote to my parents every two or three months, which delighted them. He urged me to write as well, to show off my newfound skill. Even though they could not read themselves, my parents asked the Rev. Mr Dickins to read the letters to them, which he did, and they kept them in a box as treasures.

I wrote, with the help of Mr Puttenden and Betsey, the following letter:

My dear father and
    Mother and my Love and duty to my dear brothers and sisters I hop i shall find you all in good helth Ples give my Love to grandmother and ant burgess and all friends Im in most delightful place and my mistress Treats me with all Imaginable kindness and my youn miss is Larnd me to write and ihope ishall nax Letter isen belebl to write bettr.

    befor I hve ver good friends but my dear Mother im got so fat that you wel not lard me now but I wnt to now the situation that you Live in with it is beter now and it nas when i Live there is was bad Enough so now I hop it is beter now and i hop you will send me letter to tel now how all of you are but my dear father i hop hoo will kip my deer sister fom ple for it will be the raun of her for i never did my time pass mor agreeably for i do my work wil paleasure wen i have dond reading for i never go yout yout is to church and i naver so happy as wen bmy salf but my dear mother I whe you wer so happy as im i hop my dear brothers will never let you want for ant thin I wich it was in my por to mker you comfortable but my dear mother I have send you wun pond not and I hop it wall be acceptable presents wen my dear father have got wan vever to beg of you that is you send my aged for i wich to now how hold im wich i her yous most humbly duty Loving daughter – Mary Willcocks, Mrs Mathews clapham rod place kennington November 24

Mrs Baker would thank Mrs Wilcock to call at Mr Horsefalls Linen Draper No 81 Fore-street Exeter to let her know if this safe 22 Dec. 1811
'Thomas Willcocks
Witheridge near Crediton Devon.'

Mr Puttenden, in his letter to my parents, told them what an angel Mrs Mathews had been to me. He also informed them that I was a good and willing servant, and Mrs Mathews called me their adopted child.

My parents, when they received the letters from Mr Puttenden and myself, were overjoyed, and called Mr Puttenden my Saviour.

He had so relieved their minds of worry about me, that they sent him three fat ducks and a pint of cream.

In August that year I fell ill again with the fever. Mrs Mathews nursed me. The face of God, wrathful and bearded, rose up in my imagination at night and loomed above me, telling me that I was still a sinner at heart, however good I might appear my soul was still black. Hell fire seemed very close.

As soon as I was able to write I sat up in bed and wrote a second letter to my parents.

Mary Willcocks
Mrs Mathews Claptam
road Place

Kinnington N 1 August 19 1812

My Dear Father and My Mother i hop you are wall as im im the blsed of god I have ben vary hill but Iam Much bater thank the Lord for it. Pleace to give My Duty and Love to My dear Brothers and sister and i hop they Are wall and i hop you will be so kind as to remember Me to ant Burgess and all Friends I want to Bed a favory of you would you pleace to sen me Word wre sally dinner live as I wich to see her. i have very good friends so you see i have got thee 3 Fathers ther is Mr Puttenden you Mu Dear and i hope i have got a heavenly Father I hop you will tell me of any good that may Attend you give me opportunity to rejoice hide Not from me any evil that may befal you That i may mingle My tears with yours i Bend me down with gratitude for last Paternal gift you make me which has Proved My salvation and it will add Batterness to my Years force to my groans and sharpness to the Stripe if the virtues and suffering of this life are Not sufficient to atone for the last ast of disobedience May every happiness and comfort attend you My Last Prayers in this world will Be for those that have loved me and I am your most obliged affestionate' . . .

(no signature)

At this point the fever overtook me, and I wept and blotted the page. Mrs Mathews, who had been helping me with the spelling, washed my face with cold water. I became delirious. I saw myself again as a very bad girl. When I lay down, I was unable to sit up again.

Mrs Mathews must have folded the letter up and sealed it. She wrote 'Mrs Willcocks' on it, and Mr Puttenden directed it by carrier to Exeter, to Mr Horsefells, Linen and Drapery Store, Exeter.

I made no acquaintance with anyone while I lived with Mrs Mathews and Miss Betsey. After my fever I had one outing with Mr Puttenden. As a favour, he took me to see the lady who had suggested me for the place as servant to Mrs Mathews. She was always asking after me, Mr Puttenden said, and was interested to know what had become of me. She was pleased to hear that I was doing so well, and patted my cheek and gave me sixpence.

Mrs Mathews told me she protected me against the sins and evils of the world, and I believed her.

Mr Puttenden liked to talk to me. He would follow me down the passage and into the kitchen, and tell me to continue what I was doing before I went to answer the door.

'Work is the highest form of endeavour, Mary,' he would say, 'the closest we can get to Godliness.' Often a complete passage from the Bible would follow, before he left me to take a glass of madeira wine and some seed cake with Mrs Mathews.

At such times I became irritable.

I knew it was wrong of me, but I wanted to be outside in the sunshine, listening to the birds and seeing people pass in carriages. I wanted to feel alive again.

The days ticked past, the months, the years, and the house shut me in like a prison. I only went out once in all the three years I stayed with Mrs Mathews. I was so often told how happy I must be, surrounded by luxury and well fed, that I could find no reason to complain except my own base ingratitude.

It was not until I made the acquaintance of the cook of our next door neighbours that I was undone.

The family who lived next door were Jews, and rich. One day, when hanging out our washing, I glanced over the wall.

To do so meant standing on tiptoe, but I had become intrigued by rustling sounds on the other side. My eyes met those of a stout young woman in a lace-edged cap and apron, also hanging out the washing. She looked friendly, and we exchanged smiles. I found that her name was Abigail, she could read and write, and she was the Jew's cook. She liked her employers, she told me, for her mistress gave her cast off clothes, and broken meats to sell, as part of her wages. We gossiped happily for some time, and she discovered I was becoming discontented.

After that I found her a good friend and we talked continually over the garden wall when our mistresses were not about.

If she had not come into my life, I might be with Mrs Mathews still. I was always headstrong, and unwittingly she brought about my downfall.

It happened in this way.

Abigail become concerned about my sickly pallor and listless behaviour, for I had not been well since having the fever, and was a prey to the head ache.

She said what I needed was gaiety and excitement. I must talk to other young people, such as herself. Being in the house all day was killing my spirit. She added that the Jew's only daughter was to be married at the Horns, Kennington, and it would please her if I could accompany her thither.

I resolved to go, be the consequence what it would, and asked Mrs Mathews for leave to take an afternoon off.

She was arranging her bonnet, carefully tying the strings. 'I do not think it wise,' she told me. 'You are too young and inexperienced to go out, on your own.' 'But Ma'am,' I pleaded, 'it would be for so short a time!' 'No, Mary.' She patted her hair and adjusted her gloves. 'You are alone in the world,' she added, 'you will be sure to pick up evil companions who will fill your mind with discontent. I do not like to think what the consequences could be.'

I could not believe it. It was the first time I had asked her for anything.

'You were poor and sickly when I took you in,' she continued. 'I rescued you from certain death or dishonour on the streets.' She was still tying her bonnet strings, but stopped to look hard at me. 'How could you have found another place to take you in?' she queried me. 'How could you have supported yourself in your feeble condition when you left the hospital? I am responsible for you. You owe me a great deal, Mary, and there are signs that you could be frivolous, if left to your own devices. I fear for your safety in the world outside.'

I was very hurt by her refusal, and by the fact that she did not trust me. I had done no wrong since being in her house. She had known me for three years. Was I never to be allowed out on my own?

I went down to the kitchen and cried. She did not hear my sobs. She had gone out, locking the door behind her. I dried my eyes, for crying would not help me, and planning would. I began to think. I knew I had to devise a plan to persuade Mrs Mathews to let me out of the house.

An idea came to me.

Mrs Baynes, a milliner, often visited the house. A weakness of Mrs Mathews' was a love of bonnets and hats, and she would spend many hours in front of the looking glass arranging her features, patting her hair, and trying on new shapes. Mrs Baynes was a great favourite and a most admirable and virtuous Christian. Often I was called upon to give comments, and thus quite a friendship had developed between us.

Mrs Baynes had lately lain in, and Mrs Mathews, I was sure, would sympathise if she requested my presence at the christening of her child.

I went into the garden, and, having made sure that Mrs Mathews was nowhere to be seen, I gave three taps upon the wall with a stick, which was our code, and meant 'Is all well? Have you the time to speak?' An answering three taps, I stood on tiptoe, and Abigail's eyes met mine. She had been sunning herself beneath the wall on a wooden stool brought out from the kitchen.

I explained my plan to her, and begged her to write a letter, purporting to come from Mrs Baynes, asking Mrs Mathews to let me attend the christening of her child the following afternoon, and saying how obliged she would be if the favour was granted. I told Abigail it must be a refined, persuading sort of note, and one that could not well be refused.

Abigail put the note in the post and it was received by Mrs Mathews the next morning. Fearful with anticipation I carried the note to her. She read it with great attention, not showing the least sign of suspicion. 'Mrs Baynes wishes you to attend the christening of her child,' she told me. 'It is somewhat late for her to write, for it is to be this afternoon. I am surprised that she has not given us more time to answer her – surely the christening cannot have been set up in such a hurry? Perhaps she remembered you, after her last visit, bringing my green bonnet with the feather. Or was that in the winter? I cannot remember when it was that she last came here. However,' and here Mrs Mathews twitched a curl forward over her cheek and settled her cap further forward, 'I shall allow you to attend the christening, Mary, for it will be in the church, and no harm can come to you there – and if there is a small party afterwards, why, it will be a sober and Christian one, and will not encourage vice. I know that you will come to no harm in Mrs Baynes' care. You must, however, be home at 8 in the evening and no later.'

I dressed myself in my other gown, and put a ribbon in my bonnet when out of sight of the house. Abigail was waiting for me, and we reached the wedding in high spirits. We were made much fuss of, being the only young females present, and I returned home very pleased with myself.

I was home at eight. Mrs Mathews said nothing that night, except to exclaim that I looked rosy cheeked and better than she had seen me in a long while; and she could tell from my expression that I had enjoyed myself. I told her, yes, and she said for me to go to bed, for she needed me no more that day. I retired quickly, frightened of being questioned too closely.

The next morning, while eating, she asked me the child's name. I had my mouth full and was unable to reply for a moment, which gave me time to think. 'Edward Francis, Ma'am,' I told her, when I had swallowed, but I was afraid, for I did not know if the child was a boy or girl.

'Tell me about the christening,' Mrs Mathews continued. She looked at me with great attention. 'Was it a large party? Who were the godparents? What did you have to eat and drink? Did the child cry?'

I coloured and began to stammer. Yes, it had been a pleasant enough occasion, I did not know the names of the godparents, I had talked mainly with Mrs Baynes, the child did not cry, and the Christening robe was silk and had lace trimmings. 'And what did Mrs Baynes wear?' 'O, one of her bonnets, trimmed with feathers, and a . . . a . . . yellow silk dress with a spencer.'

Mrs Mathews became suddenly silent. I did not realise at the time how deeply I had aroused her suspicions.

Mrs Mathews went to enquire of the truth of my story, and having ascertained from Mrs Baynes that I had not been invited to the christening, nor had gone, unasked, she proceeded to question all who might know of my whereabouts that afternoon.

Presently she found out the whole story, and was very angry. She scolded me very much.

On her return she desired Mr Puttenden to call, to advise her what to do with me, and called me to her to tell me of this.

I did not wait to be scolded by Mr Puttenden. In great haste I ran from the kitchen, not stopping to put on my bonnet and cloak, and waited nearby behind a tree, thinking Mr Puttenden would soon leave.

He stayed all night.

I grew so cold as I walked about the entire night in the back lane, having no bonnet or cloak; up and down, up and down, my heart sore from knowledge of my wrongdoings. I could not face Mr Puttenden's horror at my conduct.

In the morning Mrs Mathews saw me in the back lane for I did not know what to do nor where to go. She called me to her, and told me that staying out at night was an additional offence.

My head was buzzing with the noise of her scolding. Had she been kind, had she forgiven me, I would have stayed. Perhaps she wanted me to beg her pardon – but I was dumb. I packed my trunk while she stood and shouted at me. I changed into my old gown, folded up the clothes she had given me, and laid them on the kitchen table. My fingers were so numb I could scarcely use them.

She did not say goodbye to me, but I saw her as I walked down the lane. She was standing at the parlour window watching me go, and her face looked drawn and old.

A SERVICE AT THE MAGDALEN

... 'Lord Hertford, at the head of the governors with their white staves, met us at the door, and led the Prince directly into the chapel, where, before the altar, was an armchair for him, with a blue damask cushion, a prie-Dieu, and a footstool of black cloth with gold nails. We sat on forms near him. There were Lord and Lady Dartmouth in the odour of devotion, and many city ladies. The chapel is small and low, but neat, hung with Gothic paper, and tablets of benefactions. At the west end were the enclosed sisterhood, above an hundred and thirty, all in greyish brown stuffs, broad handkerchiefs, and flat straw hats, with a blue riband, pulled quite over their faces. As soon as we entered the chapel, the organ played, and the Magdalens sang a hymn in parts; you cannot imagine how well. The chapel was dressed with orange and myrtle, and there wanted nothing but a little incense to drive away the devil – or to invite him. Prayers then began, psalms and a sermon; the latter by a young clergyman, one Dodd, who contributed to the Popish idea one had imbibed, by haranguing entirely in the French style, and very eloquently and touchingly. He apostrophized the lost sheep, who sobbed and cried from their souls – so did my Lady Hertford and Fanny Pelham, till I believe the City dames took them both for Jane Shores ... ' Horace Walpole (1760)

H. F. B. Compston, *The Magdalen Hospital*

CHAPTER FIFTEEN

The Magdalen

Once more I had nowhere to go. There was a widow woman who stitched lace for cuffs and petticoats. She supplied Mrs Mathews and I knew she rented rooms. As I had some money saved I was able to find lodging with her for eight days.

The Widow Henry lived in a crowded tenement on the outskirts of the City. Wooden huts appeared overnight in the fields, and the older houses were rotting, supported by wooden posts. It was the cheapest place to stay but I had often heard it said, not entirely in jest, that London was a town where falling houses thundered on your head.

I was nervous when I found that the Widow Henry lived in the garret. She was, however, pleased to take me in, for her previous lodger had died the week before.

Our room was low-ceilinged with a leaking roof. The two small windows were never opened, for it was very cold. Though my room had been small at Mrs Mathews' I had been the sole occupant. Here, in the garret, the Widow Henry took up all the space. She was red faced and extremely big. When she moved, the floor shook, and when she sat down the bench groaned. The room smelt of sweat, mingled with the stench from the stairwell, used by the families in the building as a convenience. A carter came to collect the night-soil once a day, to use on the fields. He paid the Widow Henry a small sum for the privilege.

The Widow Henry's bed folded into the wall in the daytime, leaving room for a table, at which she worked. The bed was so small that when my landlady had coughed herself to sleep I could not turn over. Rain came through the roof, Drip! Drip! Drip! into a bucket.

I had nothing to do but look for work, and there was none to be had.

The Widow Henry was drinking herself into a stupor, both to keep warm and to keep her fears at bay. The lace making was causing her to go blind.

Life was so dreadful to her, she appeared to be drinking herself to death to spite it. I was sorry for her, but there was little I could do.

Because I did not know what I was going to do, I asked the Widow Henry to write to my father, telling him that I had left Mrs Mathews, and sending him my clothes in the trunk. I thought it would please him if I asked her to mention that I had left England with a travelling family.

I decided to become a nun. It seemed so simple. If I could stop being wicked and having wicked thoughts, and curb my headstrong ways, I would be fed and looked after all my life. I was worried about being always good – I was vain and had a great love of finery. Would it be possible NOT to sin? I did not know. The lesson life had taught me was that all the nice things in life brought only trouble. Surely in a Nunnery I would find it easy to be good?

There was a high walled brick building in Blackfriars Road, called the Magdalen. The gates were always locked when I passed, but I fancied it was a Nunnery. I asked the Widow Henry if she thought I could enter the Magdalen, and if they would have me? She replied 'Surely Mary, you do not want to go there?' I told her I did, I was serious in my intention, I simply wondered if they took in servant girls, such as myself. She said Yes, they took women of all types. I asked when it was possible to go inside? She told me the first Wednesday in a month.

I wanted to try what being a nun would be like.

The next Wednesday, which was the first in the month, I walked to the Magdalen. The building looked so much like a prison from the outside that I almost regretted my decision, but I could not see what else I could do.

As I stood watching, a child in a red straw bonnet with draggle feathers and a scarlet satin petticoat two sizes too large for her came timidly along the street and knocked on the door. She hung back when the door was opened. but someone pulled her inside.

My heart was beating so loudly I thought everyone must hear it. I felt sick, and very cold for I had not eaten for two days. Summoning up courage, I knocked. The door was opened by a young girl in a pretty print dress and apron, with a cap lined with lace. She gestured for me to go into the hall which was full of women. All ages, all shapes. Some old and ugly, some young and pretty. Many were children. They all looked cold and hungry and pinched, and they smelt dreadful, as, I expect, I did. One or two were drunk, and sprawled along the bench, and I looked at them with horror, for how could these poor drunk women hope to become nuns? Or the children? Surely, to be a nun, you needed to be of a certain age?

Our bonnets and caps were taken off and thrown into a heap in the corner. We were summoned, one by one, into an inner room, behind whose thick oak doors came the murmur of voices, and sometimes a cry, or a burst of sobbing. When the door re-opened some women carried slips of paper and looked happy, others were empty handed and desperate.

When my turn came I was trembling so much I could hardly walk. The door closed behind me, and when I looked round I was in a dark panelled room, lined with portraits. Behind a table at the far end of the room sat a clergyman with a long face and white hair, a stout, white-faced woman in a starched cap and apron, and several gentlemen of quality. There were no nuns.

The lady in uniform spoke first. She was the matron, Mrs Elizabeth Wiggins. The clergyman was the Chaplain to the Magdalen, Mr Prince. The other gentlemen were the committee.

'How long have you been going on in this way?' asked Mrs Wiggins. Her voice was severe. I did not know what she meant.

'Have you been long on the Town?' asked the Chaplain. When I still did not answer – for I did not know what to reply – he became impatient. 'Come, come girl, answer us!'

'You cannot pretend to be so modest,' the Matron told me, 'else you would not have come.'

They all stared at me, and began to lecture me in such a serious way that I became scarlet and could not think. I began to cry, telling them that I was sorry, I had many faults, I was wicked, I had been tempted by the Devil.

They watched me as I sobbed. The Chaplain enquired if I could give up my former life, or if I was so deep a sinner that I would find it impossible to lead a sober and decent life. I shook my head at this, and he asked me, 'Do you repent your former sins?' I nodded very fervently, but could not reply for I was crying too loudly.

They told me, as I was so young, if I was truly penitent they would take me in, which my tears prevented me from answering. One of them said, 'Poor thing, she is very much affected.' Another voice said, 'It appears she has suffered much, poor girl, see how she cries!' A third gentleman murmured, 'She seems a gentle sort of country girl,' and another added, 'It is always those from the country who suffer most.'

The Matron asked, 'shall we admit her, gentlemen?' 'She appears to be in a state of penitence, and would reward our endeavours,' the Clergyman replied.

'We will admit you,' he told me. I tried to stop my sobbing in order to thank them, and received a slip of paper with ADMITTED on it. I was ordered to deliver it to the next room. After this I was taken to a bath and all my clothes stripped from me. They scrubbed me clean and inspected my head for lice, then my hair was cut short to prevent insects lodging there, and I was dressed in the Magdalen dress, which was a stuff gown of blue with a white tippet and white apron. A plain bordered cap adorned my shorn hair, pleated round the face.

I did not feel at all like a nun, but thought that perhaps these were the clothes of a novice. They were neat and pretty and I was delighted with them.

Now, I thought, all my troubles were over. I was to be taken care of for the rest of my life, and there would be no more opportunity to sin.

I was at the Magdalen six months, during which time I acted as a sort of housemaid. Our duties as probationers were to learn how to scrub, cook and sew, knit stockings, make linen and do bead work. Some of the these occupations did not seem very religious, but I did not know any better so I never questioned them. During the time I was there I was confirmed by the Bishop. It was a very exciting moment, and I began to feel deeply devout and glad that I was now a true member of the church. The Bishop told Mr Prince, the Chaplain, that he was pleased with my behaviour, which been both modest and seemly. I was surprised. Surely, I thought, if we were about to become nuns, he could not expect us to act in any other way?

It was a pleasant life. Food was plentiful, and we ate roast beef and potatoes on Sunday, with plum pudding to follow. Bread was short, but this did not worry us. We had warm shawls to wear when the weather was cold, and were expected to look attractive at all times, being allowed to grow our hair again once it was free of lice. Our Sunday clothes were delightful. We wore a delicate light-brown dress with a white tippet folded across the bosom, and flat straw hats. I enjoyed Sundays. We all sang so sweetly in the chapel, and people came to watch us, and Mr Prince spoke feelingly about our sins. His face was benevolent but his voice boomed so wonderfully loud across the chapel as he lectured us, that we were hard put to it not to drown him with our sobs.

I became increasingly puzzled by the Magdalen. The windows in the wards had been blacked over to prevent people seeing in. This was understandable, for here we dressed and undressed and performed our ablutions. The windows were overlooked by a tall, soot-covered building nearby, which had housed a riding school and now sheltered the Surrey Theatre. From the theatre people looked down into the wards and shouted obscenities. But why did they throw letters over the wall, asking us to meet them? Why did they call out the names of some of my fellow Magdalens, from the street below? The girls would blush, and pretend not to hear, but they seemed to *expect* this sort of attention.

It was strange to me. I wondered that no one commented on such happenings.

It was common to hear bad language coming up from the streets, for the

The Magdalen Chapel in 1808

area outside the hospital had just been built over, and the neighbourhood was rough. No lady visitor stayed in the spare room of the Magdalen, for the swearing was deeply offensive. The children slept on the far side of the house for the same reason. Yet, interspersed among the oaths came the names of my fellow probationers.

I became gradually conscious that the Magdalen was not what I had supposed it to be. The inmates were so young – about a seventh part of them were not yet fifteen, and several were under fourteen. I was among the oldest of the one hundred and eleven girls. Why should nuns be admitted so young?

One day, when I was scrubbing the steps behind a pillar, I overheard two of my companion Magdalens speaking together about their former life.

The first one, whom I saw to be Etty Jennet, a red-head and very pretty, said, quite loud, so that I heard it distinctly, 'I never kept count of the men I have laid with. Though I do truly repent that I did so, and pleasant though this place be, and comfortable, I am bored.' 'Shush, Etty,' said her companion, an idle slut of a girl named Kate, 'shush, we will be overheard.'

Etty continued, nonetheless. 'If a gentleman (with reasonable appearance) came to me now, and promised me lodgings and a silk petticoat, why, Lord, I think I would succumb. I could not answer for myself. And two silk petticoats, or a shawl and a pair of stockings, or slippers made of kid leather . . . ,' she pushed her hands through her red hair and gave a sigh.

'Oh Kate, can you not see him? Blue eyes, blue as the sea. Tall, and dark, with a noble brow and well formed nose. It is an exquisite picture, Kate. Why cannot I meet him now?'

'You are in the Magdalen,' warned Kate, 'thinking those thoughts shows that you are in no way repentant. Mr Prince would be much upset if he thought you were still hungering after your wicked ways.'

'Stuff Mr Prince!' cried Etty. 'Oh Etty, be quiet,' said Kate, 'he is a nice man, and he pities us in our condition. I came to this place after my illness. I had expected to be kept by an old gentleman who loved me to distraction and called me his poppet (I went to him when I was twelve). He said he would leave me money to live on, but when he died his relations came to the house and took everything. I was turned into the street, and could not find employment, for I was big with child. It was fortunate the child died at birth, else I do not know what I would have done. I was so ill, Etty, I wished to die myself. And so I came here, and they have been very good to me.'

'YOU have suffered' replied Etty, 'and I am heartily sorry for you. But I am full of life, and promise, and do not wish to waste my life as servant to some finicking old lady, locked in a cold damp house with shutters shut tight. I want to live, Kate to live! And if living means becoming a whore once again, then go back to whoring I shall!'

I could not believe what I was hearing. I came out from behind the pillar, dropping my scrubbing brush with a clatter to the floor and the girls jumped round guiltily.

'Surely,' I asked them, 'surely only prostitutes lie with men? What do you mean, when you say you will go back to whoring? Where you really a whore? How came you to be in a nunnery?' I looked from one to the other. 'How came you to be here?'

They laughed so much at this that I thought they would die. They clung to each other and gasped with mirth, tears ran down their faces and they whooped and hiccupped as though demented.

'You ARE a simpleton,' they told me. 'How is it, after so many weeks, you have not understood? You MUST be as bad as we are – how else could you have gained admittance to the house?'

I began to cry. 'I have not sinned in THAT way,' I replied through my sobs. 'I have never lain with any man. I am ashamed that you should think it of me.'

They did not believe me and became angry. 'What do you know of the Bible?' asked Etty. 'What does the name Magdalen mean to you? Can you really be so ignorant? The hymns we sing in chapel, the sermons that are directed at us, the prayers we say, how *can* you not have realised, all this time, that we are prostitutes?'

'Those big, innocent eyes,' scoffed Kate, pointing, 'that simple air – ' she stared into my face 'don't deceive me ONE BIT. You knew it all the time. You wanted somewhere to sleep and someone to feed you. You are *worse* than we are. You have lied and cheated to come here. You have duped Mr Prince, and done another, worthier girl out of the place.'

'O leave her be,' said Etty, shaking her head. 'But she has done so well out of the Magdalen,' cried Kate, 'working her way into Mr Prince's good graces, yes sir, no sir, and Mr Prince so taken in – yes sir I am a wicked girl, sir, but through you I will win grace in the eyes of the Lord – I heard you – Mr Prince believes he has converted a sinner and Lord, Lord, she was no sinner at all.' Kate laughed harshly. 'He thought you were a sweet country girl, newly seduced in London – he made a pet of you, didn't he, Mary? Because he thought he had snatched you from the streets and saved your soul.'

Etty shrugged. 'She had better go and discuss the matter with Mr Prince,' she said. 'The Magdalen does not keep anyone who used not to be a prostitute. If you want to stay,' she added, turning and looking me full in the face, 'you had better go out and sin. They're out there, waiting, ready to fall upon the first girl to leave through the gates. Go on Mary, go out and sin!'

Kate snorted, and together, arm in arm, they left me. I passed them, laughing in the corridor with a group of Magdalens. I knew that they were talking about me.

I went to find Mr Prince, to vindicate myself. I did not want to be thought a prostitute. He was in the chapel, arranging his sermon in the pulpit, ready for the evening service.

I did not know how to approach him, and sat for a while in a pew, watching him. At length he beckoned me to him. 'Is there something troubling you?' he asked in a kindly voice. I began to cry again. 'Come, come,' he remonstrated, 'tell me the matter. I have some minutes before the service, and can listen to you.' He smiled encouragingly. I continued to sob. At length he put his hand on my arm and led me from the chapel and into a small room adjoining. Here he sat down, and told me to sit.

'Are you unwell?' he asked me. 'Has someone been unkind? Are you teased? Have you hurt yourself?' 'No, no,' I sobbed, 'there is nothing wrong with me but I have been stupid. I am sorry, I am so sorry, I do not know how it came about, but I thought the Magdalen was a Nunnery, I never thought it was for prostitutes, or I would not have come.' I cried more loudly. Mr Prince jumped as though a wasp had stung him.

'A Nunnery?' His voice was angry. 'A *Nunnery?*' 'Yes sir, if it please you, sir,' I sniffed. 'You MUST have been aware that the Magdalen was a home for reformed prostitutes!' he exclaimed. 'You cannot be so simple! I do not believe you. It is *impossible* that you did not know! When you were asked questions about your former life, you replied you were sorry for your sins!'

His face had reddened and his eyes seemed to flash fire. I was afraid to look at him. 'How *could* you think this was a Nunnery!' he repeated, staring at me. He looked at me with horror. 'Can you really be so stupid?' He paused, and passed his hand over his face wearily, as though he did not wish to understand what I was saying. 'How *could* you fail to know that this is a home for penitents? Is it possible to be so deaf and blind that you can live among prostitutes for six months and think them all nuns?'

He sent for Mrs Wiggins after the service, and the committee was convened to discuss my fate.

When I was summoned before them again their faces were so stern I could not look at them. They lectured me on my deception, telling me that some woman who desperately needed the help of the Magdalen might have been turned away for my sake, that I had cheated my way into the house, and could not stay a moment longer.

They delivered my clothes to me, and a pound note which was in the pocket of my dress when I went in.

As soon as I had changed my clothes I was shown to the door and found myself in the street. The gates of the Magdalen shut behind me.

EVIDENCE OF THE
POLICE COMMITTEE HELD AT THE
HOUSE OF COMMONS, 1816

Q. 'The activity of the Bow Street Officers has infinitely increased of late years?'

A. (Townshend, a Bow Street Runner) 'No doubt about it, sir. We used to have ten or fifteen highway robberies a week, we have not had one lately. I mean persons on horseback, on Hounslow Heath, Wimbledon, or Finchley Commons. Now people travel safely by means of the new horse-patrol.'

Q. 'Do you think any advantages arise from a man being gibbeted after execution?'

A. 'Yes, I was always of that opinion. Say two men are hanging by the roadside, folk say, "why, these are hung and gibbeted for robbing on the highway", so the thing is kept alive. If it was not for this robbers would die and nobody know anything of it. But where we hanged five highwaymen, say in 1788, we only hang one now!'

Gordon S. Maxwell, Highwayman's Heath

CHAPTER SIXTEEN

I Fall among Highwaymen

I thought of going to the country to visit my father and mother, whom I had not seen for a long time. Instead of going directly, being afraid of walking over Hounslow Heath on account of the robberies and murders that took place there, I decided to change into a man.

The wind always blew in a sinister fashion over the heath. There was nothing for miles but coarse grass, copses of tall trees, winding paths leading nowhere, thick woods, and black swampy ponds in whose weed-covered water I expected to see a dead body. The road over the heath was lined with gibbets, often bearing a corpse, sometimes in chains, and these chains screamed and groaned as if the corpse was alive and lamenting his position. I believed that when the wind howled and the moon was full, ghosts came out on the heath. Some ghosts had no heads, and some rode horses whose eyes flashed fire. Jerry Abershawe, only recently executed, climbed down from his gibbet to seek revenge, and he was a terrible man! He was seen only in moonlight, and then the flash of steel as he drew his sword gave him away. Ghosts could kill, I had been told so by someone who knew. When Jerry was hanged outside Newgate prison, twenty thousand people came to see the sight, and some tumbled, and others fell over them, until there were two or three heaps of persons on the ground, trying to extricate themselves. Three women died, and two boys, and the injured were carried off in carts.

I had heard of Cutpurse Moll, a woman turned highwayman, who changed into men's clothes as soon as she was old enough, and never afterwards wore petticoats. It seemed to me to be a sensible idea to become a boy. I could then walk fast and carry a stick, and speak in a gruff voice, and if I dressed poorly, no one would want to rob me. My figure was slight and boyish, and my hair still short.

I discovered a pawnbroker's shop down an alley off the Blackfriars Road. Going inside I bargained for men's clothes in exchange for mine. For my dress and bonnet, the old pawnbroker gave me a long straight drab coat, light coloured stockings, a neckcloth and some boots. The jacket was musty and had been home to a family of mice, so that I smelt of droppings. The breeches were darned and patched and little of the original material remained, but sensing my anger at being so fobbed off in return for my good clothes, the old man threw in a tattered greatcoat to keep me warm. The boots had stout soles and seemed comfortable and dry.

Seeing my delight at changing to a man, and the way I strutted and tried to see myself, to know what impression I would make, the old pawnbroker gave me powder for my hair, which I put on, and combed it, and took the earrings out of my ears. 'You look a brave young man indeed,' he told me, 'you'll be lucky if you're not hanged by evening.'

'Is my voice too high?' I asked him, trying to pitch it lower. He cackled and said I was so young, with no beard showing, that a falsetto would not come amiss. I tried to become husky, and he said my voice would do, I would pass as a youth. I walked up and down and he cried, 'Good! Very Good! Remember if you are in trouble you must not scream!' I assured him I would not. 'Use your fists and feet and keep quiet,' he advised me. I told him I wished to avoid trouble and he chuckled and blew his nose on his neckcloth.

To try whether my sex would be detected I went to a house to see if there was a vacancy for a young man. At the first house they laughed at me for being so very short a man, but at the second I was introduced to three gentlemen and four ladies, playing cards in a dark room full of ornaments.

In the corner I saw a pale face and fingers beckoning. Mrs Mumford was a birdlike woman with a curious pecking motion of the head, like a hen drinking. She eyed me frankly through her lorgnette while the gentlemen held up quizzing glasses.

Mrs Mumford enquired my age. I said I thought I was twenty, but did not know. One of the gentlemen drawled, 'He is so little a man, he will give but little pleasure,' and laughed. The ladies tittered with him and called him a Wag. 'What have you done in the past?' they asked me.

I said I had been footman, gardener, coachman and valet. 'You have changed places many times?' asked Mrs Mumford. 'No,' I replied, and she looked puzzled. 'It was for the same family,' I told her. 'Gadzooks!' cried the Wag, 'It appears he is a very Paragon among men.' 'But where is your reference?' asked Mrs Mumford. I replied that I had lost it while travelling. 'I can do anything,' I assured her, and at this the gentlemen were laughing and winking at each other, as though I had made a lewd remark. Perhaps I might show them my skills as they had time to spare, and again they cried with laughter.

After a while they became bored with quizzing me, but they never suspected I was not a young man. Mrs Mumford began to yawn, and said there was a strange odour in the room, she did not know where from, but it was making her faint. The gentleman nearest her began to fan her violently, while another waved his handkerchief in the air and cried 'Faugh! It is a farmyard smell!' 'Let us go back to cards,' they said, 'we have been interrupted long enough.'

Mrs Mumford waved for me to go. 'There is nothing here you can do for me,' she snapped. 'I will not take you into my service, you are too little a youth, and you look so very wicked.'

'He is the sort of rogue who will steal the silver teaspoons on his way out,' drawled a lady in pink.

It seemed better not to reply.

After that I set off home in earnest, having bought a pasty to nourish me on the journey.

I crossed Hounslow Heath in safety, seeing no ghosts and no highwaymen. I slept at night in ditches, protected by hedges, and moved on when it was light.

The heath was fearsome. Between two roads, behind a clump of firs, stood a gibbet on which hung two bodies in chains. The iron plates scarcely kept the gibbet together, and the rags of the highwaymen displayed their horrible skeletons. A scattering of crows was pecking at the remains.

One night I spent at the Green Man at Hatton, where a friendly ostler let me lie in the stables. There was a hole in the back of the fireplace, he told me, where highwaymen hid. It was pitch black and often hot, but they were never smoked out by the Excise Men. Afterwards they could be heard for miles, coughing and spluttering from the effects of the smoke on their lungs.

On Salisbury Plain my troubles began. Two men on horseback overtook me, and stopped in front of me on the path, so that I could not move.

'Have you any money?' asked one. He was tall and elegant, in a scarlet coat, green waistcoat, white stockings and laced hat. In his hand he carried a pistol. His companion was dressed in black and both wore masks.

I decided to be impudent.

'No,' I answered, 'I was hoping YOU would give ME money.' They laughed at this. 'He appears a rascal,' they told each other. They looked at me with interest. 'You have no work?' they enquired. 'No,' I replied, 'I am begging my way along the road, and I am hungry.' 'Are you seeking a place?' 'I might be,' I said, 'if it is a good place.' 'Perhaps you would go with us, and enter into our service?' they asked me.

I did not know what to reply. To say no might have meant instant death. To say yes – it was an adventure, but a frightening one.

The pistol before my eyes, I asked them, innocently, what I would do for them? 'You would look after our horses when we come home, and go out with us by night,' they told me.

'Where do you go to?' I said. They looked at each other. 'We will not tell you now, it would be dangerous for us, you might prove a spy sent by the Runners. If you are found faithful, we will tell you, then you must become a member of our company.'

I accepted their offer, determined to find out their business, and persuaded by their pistols.

They led me through a maze of trackways with swamps on either side of the path and clumps of bent trees, deformed by the wind. One man led the way and the other walked beside me on his horse. They did not talk to me, but I heard muttered remarks. 'Take care, the path is treacherous here,' or, 'That fellow we saw back there in chains – I could swear it was Ned Deane.' I said nothing, for I was afraid.

After a time we came to a small house in the heath, a tumbledown, haunted, desolate place, surrounded by tall thorn hedges, impossible to see until you stumbled across it in the wilderness.

They made me sit on a settle by the fire and gave me rum and hot water to drink, for they told me I looked cold and ill.

After we had been there an hour, four more men came in. They enquired if I was to be trusted, and one of them threw a bloodstained bag of clothing on the floor and said he had had to kill to get even as little as that – an old greatcoat and a pair of boots – there was no money to be had.

Another asked if we had heard the story of the girl stripped naked and tied to a tree? Her assailants had not ravished her, but they had taken everything she had, down to her garters. She was rescued by a Dragoon who happened to hear her cries of lament. The Dragoon took her to a public house to warm her (laughter broke out at this point), but on entering they discovered the villains who had treated her so badly, toasting their ill gotten gains in wine! And telling all the company how they had come by the money to treat themselves!

The conversation then turned to the state of the weather, being good only for politicians, women and witches, as it was so changeable.

Then one of them began a ghost story which so intrigued me I listened intently. It happened in Hammersmith Churchyard. Every night at full moon something white rose up from the graves and crossed the churchyard howling and moaning, terrible to hear. It frightened the whole village. One night a young married woman, big with child, crossed the churchyard. The ghost caught her up in its arms – and she swooned away. Later both she and the child died. The next full moon her husband hid in the churchyard, and when he saw an apparition all in white come towards him, he raised his shotgun and fired. The Thing gave a loud groan and fell, but the husband, going closer, observed the apparition to be none other than the wheelwright taking a short cut home through the churchyard. Of course, the husband was tried for murder, and executed.

The men began to ask me questions. How old was I? What had I been doing before I was apprehended on Salisbury Plain? Where was I going? Was I an apprentice, run away, or had I finished my apprenticeship? If so, what was it? What sort of work could I do? Did I have a mother or father, relations or friends, who would want to know my whereabouts? I answered cautiously, and was surprised that none of them doubted my being a young man.

One man asked, 'Can you fire a pistol?' 'No,' I said, 'I have never learnt.' 'Then you must begin at once,' answered the captain. 'You will be of no use to us until you can.' He beckoned me into the yard, and the men followed. 'Here,' said the captain, taking a pistol, 'I will show you how this works, and then you must fire it. We will not be too hard on you – your first target can be the hay bale over there, which should be impossible to miss!'

Indeed, the hay bale looked comfortingly large. The loading of the pistol was a lengthy and dangerous task. The captain took a steel charger and filled it to the brim with gunpowder, then primed the pan, putting the remainder of the powder in the barrel of the gun. He rammed in the wadding, but warned me to hold the ramrod loosely between finger and thumb and not jam the wadding in too hard, for the pistol might explode.

He added I must not fire the gun until I had taken care that the flask of gunpowder was out of reach of sparks. Several of his friends, he said, had been blown up by the flask igniting.

When he handed me the pistol I was shaking so much I could hardly hold it, and my teeth chattered together in such a way I was sure they would all hear it.

'When I give the order, fire!' he told me. The men scattered as though fearing for their lives, and watched me closely. 'Fire!' he shouted, 'and mind you hit the hay bale!'

I shut my eyes, but could not pull the trigger.

'He is a chicken,' said one of the men, 'he will be no use to us.' What ails the lad?' called out another, 'He can scarcely stand for fright!' 'I have never seen so great a coward,' chirruped a third, 'he cannot even bring himself to fire at a hay bale!'

I was so angry I fired. There was a searing pain in my arm and I felt as though I had been shaken to pieces. The noise of the explosion ran right through me.

'Murder!' I screamed 'I am murdered!' I dropped the pistol and sank to the ground, convinced that I had been hit.

The scream gave me away.

'A woman!' they cried out, 'It's a woman.' In an instant they surrounded me, threatening to destroy me if I did not tell them the truth. Had I been sent as a spy by the Bow Street Runners? A great clatter broke out in the stables where the horses had been frightened by the noise. Some of the men went to calm them while the others set to in a fierce argument as to whether I should be hanged or not. A bald-headed robber was hit over the back of the head with a stick for defending me, but, turning on his opponent, he trounced him until the blood flowed. A third doused the pair of them with a bucket of muddy water from the stables.

'No good comes with a woman,' yelled a young man, and was told to remember his mother, and said he did, and regretted it, and the battle went on around me, and I, the cause of it all, lay, numb with horror, unable to move out of the way.

Suddenly the captain shouted,'You fools! be 'ee mad? Brawling at a time like this! Shall we hang the wench or no?' There was a sudden silence. I clambered to my knees to beg pardon, clutching at the captain's knees, though he tried to kick me off.

I said I had dressed as a man to escape attention, rather than draw it down upon me. Why *should* I spy on them? A girl dressed as a man – surely the Bow Street Runners would have better spies than I – they would have sent a man who WAS a man – they would have had more sense than to send a woman – the risk of discovery was too great – I was innocent, simply begging my way home, for I had no money and I was trying to avoid trouble. I only wished to see my father and mother again.

I knelt there, hands upraised, the picture, I hoped of pitiful innocence. They listened until I had finished, then a voice said 'I would not wish to kill her,' and another voice took up the refrain, until they all swore they had no wish to destroy me. The captain begged me to stop my tears, for they were reminding him of some uncomfortable encounters with women in the past. He added that I should get to my feet.

I told them if they would free me, I would never tell anybody in the world about them. And I have not, until now. The captain drew his sword and said, 'If you will swear by this sword and all the Powers Above, that you will never betray us, we will let you go free.'

This I did, with the greatest goodwill in the world.

The captain felt in his breeches pocket and drew out a guinea, which he gave me, wishing me godspeed upon my journey. He added, he hoped no further harm would befall me. I dried my tears and thanked him, and wished them all well. One of the men fished in his pocket and added five shillings to my guinea, and with so much money in my pocket I felt happy again.

The captain set me back on the road to Exeter and nothing of interest happened for the rest of the journey home.

I arrived at Witheridge in men's clothes, much to the amazement of my father and mother, who did not recognise me and asked me who I was.

When I told them it was Mary, come home to see them, they were much surprised, thinking that I was away with a travelling family.

I told them that I had left the family and asked my father if he had received my trunk, which I had sent home from London? My father said Yes, the trunk had arrived. He gave me back my clothes, so that I could dress as a woman again.

I missed the freedom I had felt in men's clothes, and the fun of putting on different manners to make the disguise believable, and the way young women had looked at me, as though I was a fine fellow.

My parents wished me to stay near home, so that they could visit me. I agreed to this, thinking I had had enough of adventures for the moment.

My mother had heard of a place for me at Crediton, with a Mr Pring, a tanner, who was looking for a willing girl to help with the work. I lived there three months. Carts came daily into the yard loaded with skins, and I was obliged to pull the hides out of the cart and carry them across the yard to the curing shed. The smell of the skins, and the weight, and the blood dripping across the yard as I carried them, made me sick. The dog dung used for curing the hides smelt most horrible. The place was dreadful to me. The smell was always in my nostrils and my clothes and I could not rid myself of it. At the end of the three months I gave in my notice and left.

I did not wish to anger my parents by telling them I had left my place, so I walked to Latford, and there I heard of a place several miles off, at a little village named Spring (near Calne). Here I hired myself, and stayed several months. My mistress was a farmer's wife, a pleasant, hearty woman.

It was the severest winter we had ever known. Snow fell continuously from January to March, cutting us off completely at the farm. We saw no living soul for weeks. The snow was so deep we could not go out. We killed and ate most of our stock of poultry and provisions, and began to suffer from deprivation. It became necessary if we were to survive, that one of us would have to set out for the market at Calne.

One morning Mrs Brownjohn called to me and said that the sky was a brilliant blue, she had seen birds flying and it looked as though the snow might be melting. If I wrapped up warmly she was sure I would reach the market. I put on two flannel petticoats, one red, one blue, coarse woollen stockings, a linen shift, a black stuff dress, a wool jacket bodice, a red woollen cloak and Mr Brownjohn's greatcoat. My head was covered by a black bonnet, with a brim stuck out in front to protect my face from the snow. Mrs Brownjohn lent me a pair of men's top boots, which were much too big for me. 'Now do 'ee take care, deary,' she called after me, 'the snow be mighty treacherous and we don't wish to lose 'ee!'

I staggered out through the yard, rolling like a boiled pudding in a kettle, so trussed up and unwieldy it was difficult to move.

Mrs Brownjohn told me to stay within sight of several landmarks; a tall oak, a coppice on the skyline, a misshapen yew tree, and one or two gate posts which stuck out from the drifts.

I was scarcely out of sight of the farm before I lost my bearings. I could not tell in which direction Calne lay. Clouds came over and hid the sun. It began to snow again and I was soon enclosed in a thick white mist. The wind lashed my face and tugged at my greatcoat as I floundered on. My eyelashes stuck together with cold. I could not tell in which direction I was walking. The country was white on all sides of me, and my footprints filled with snow.

When I turned to retrace my steps back to the farm, I found the snow had obliterated all traces of them. My foot slipped, and I fell heavily. It must have been a snowdrift in a ditch, for when I struggled to rise I sank deeper in. The snow was so soft and yielding I could not fight my way out. Each time I moved, becoming more and more panic struck, I sank deeper. At last I could not move at all. Darkness fell, and the sky cleared. The moon shone down as I struggled against sleep, fixing my eyes on the sky, pinching myself to keep awake, counting and recounting the stars. I was frightened that once I fell asleep I would never wake again. There was no sign of life in the moonlight; no hooting of owls or dogs barking. It was as though I was alone in the world. No one came to rescue me.

It was morning before they found me. Mr Brownjohn's dog scented me and helped to dig me out, so Mr Brownjohn assured me afterwards. The farmer thought I was dead, I was so white and cold. When the dog licked my face my eyelids fluttered, and putting his hand on my bosom, the farmer could just feel the beating of my heart. He said my first words, when I opened my eyes and saw the dog, were, 'I am dead.' I cannot remember it.

Mr Brownjohn carried me back to the farmhouse and Mrs Brownjohn put me to bed with hot bricks wrapped in flannel placed all round me to warm my body. I was given hot possets every few hours, and brandy, and I recovered, but after that I could not bear the country any more.

LONDON GUIDE BOOK (1778)

'A word of advice to young women as may arrive strangers in town . . . immediately on their arrival . . . and sometimes sooner, even upon the road to it, there are miscreants of both sexes on the watch to seduce the fresh country maiden, with infinite protestations of friendship, service, love and pity, to prostitution . . . For this reason, the very carriages which convey them are hunted and examined; the inns where they alight are beset by these infernal hirelings who . . . put on the demure show of modesty and sanctity for their deception. If she applies to an office of intelligence, 'tis odds but she falls into the hands of some procuress . . . '

Dorothy George, *London Life in the 18th century*

CHAPTER SEVENTEEN

I am Married

I returned to Exeter after this and enquired for service. I was at Attorney Sandford's in Goldsmith Street for three months, as cook, but I found myself at the mercy of a monstrous kitchen stove which belched smoke and was so difficult and disagreeable I could not boil a kettle without covering myself in smuts. They brought the chimney sweep to clean it, and his boy went up the chimney with his brushes, but though he scraped himself raw (and cried a great deal, for which I was sorry and gave him an apple), after they had gone it smoked just as badly as before.

At the end of the three months I gave warning and left, receiving my full wages in payment for my work.

I was restless to be gone from Exeter. It was small, and the country dull. I resolved to try London again and walked there once more, without misadventure. I did not tell my parents I was going.

I found lodgings in Billingsgate, and here, at Mrs Hillier's, a fishmonger of Darkhouse Lane, Billingsgate, I found romance.

Mrs Hillier had fiery red hair and a temper to go with it. She could swear as well as any man, and her large red hands were so powerful I have seen her knock a drunken fisherman out. She was often taken for a man in petticoats. She smelt of fish and was so fond of eels she could eat several dozen at one sitting. The Dutch eel boat captains loved her, and saved their best eels for her.

We bought fish from the market in the early morning when the boats came in, and took it straight to our stall, where we stood crying 'Fish for sale! Lovely fresh Fish for Sale!' until it was all bought. Mrs Hillier complained my voice was too soft and ladylike. She spent many hours training me to shout as raucously as she did; but it strained my throat and I could never manage it properly.

When the fish was sold we wrapped it in paper we bought in bulk from the stationers, and handed it over in a surprise parcel – sometimes a lawyer's briefs, sometimes a love letter, a mildewed verse in Latin, or a page from a novel. One day I became so engrossed in several pages of a torn novel, and was so deep in imagining myself the heroine, Pamela, that Mrs Hillier lost her temper with me and clouted me over the ear, tearing the page out of my hands and shouting that reading should be left to the gentry. Who did I think I was, filling my head with fantasy and dreaming – the poor would starve unless they stopped such nonsense and earned their daily bread. But this did not stop me reading in secret. When we ran out of paper I was sent to the stationers for more, and sometimes I stuffed a page or two down the front of my bodice to read later. That was how I met John Henry Beckerstedt.

He was *so* handsome! *So* polite! Such a dark, interesting face, and such flashing brown eyes! His fingernails were clean and his knotted handkerchief tied elegantly round his neck, and I loved him so much that the sun shone whenever I saw him.

He was leaning against the door of the stationer's booth when I entered. He stared at me so intently that I became nervous, and hesitated in my bargaining. When I had bought the paper, I stuffed a few pages, which looked interesting, down the front of my bodice, then gathered up the rest in my arms.

Looking up, I caught his eyes. I did not know if he had seen me secrete the pages away, but I blushed. Turning to leave, I dropped the papers on the floor. Bending to pick them up I looked at him, and he leant down eagerly to help. Can you imagine my dismay when the sheets of paper I had tucked down my bodice fell out upon the floor, narrowly missing his face? He looked astonished. Then he laughed – the most musical, delightful sound. He asked me, 'Can you read then? This is not paper for wrapping solely?' 'No sir,' I told him, breathlessly, 'no, sir, I can read, and enjoy it.' 'I envy its resting place,' he said, his eyes flattering me. 'If I could only nestle my head where that ungrateful paper has been lying!'

I blushed red hot and almost ran from the shop. I had been often complimented, and had learnt to answer pertly but I wanted so much for him to think well of me.

I was wearing a flat straw hat with a ribbon, and a striped dress with an apron. I knew I looked my best. My dress was bunched up, to avoid the mud of the streets, and my ankles are well shaped.

His eyes followed me, I could feel them, when I left the booth.

I heard afterwards that when I had gone he acted like one demented, demanding to know every little detail about me, what my name was, where I lived, what was my occupation. Even my age! In this way he discovered that I worked for Mrs Hillier. In the evening I received a letter from him, requesting to be allowed to see me. A few minutes later another letter came. Then a bunch of flowers.

He had been a sailor, and was just released from his ship. He stepped with great lightness of foot and gracefulness, treading in a dancing way as though on board ship still with the deck rolling beneath him. He dressed like a gentleman, but with the careless elegance of a sailor, his jacket always open, showing his strong brown neck. His hair was long and tied back in a heavy pigtail. He wore white stockings and blue trousers, and his hat was new, set well back on his head. He had a devil-may-care look about him, and a dangerous glint in his eye when he saw something he wanted. And he wanted me. He had saved all the money from his voyages and now he wanted to spend it. Everything he saw, he bought; silk stockings, a flute, handkerchiefs, gingerbread, a footman's laced hat (which he made me wear on an outing), bear's grease to make his hair grow even longer, and sweetmeats. He told me long stories about his travels. A black king had asked to be taught how to make trowsers, promising him a house and slaves if he did so; a crocodile had pursued him up a river bank and across a field. He loved to frighten me by turning up with a strange mask on his face, which he had bargained for among savages.

Frequently he called to see me when Mrs Hillier was absent. He took me to Vauxhall, where he paid one shilling each for our entrance and told me, 'Now I have such a pretty girl on my arm, I am intent on spoiling her!'

Vauxhall was magical. Everywhere lights shone in the trees like fireflies, lighting up the branches. In the middle of a little wood was a stage on which a crowd of musicians strummed and sang. When we had tired of wandering round and admiring the crowd, we sat at a table in an alcove and drank wine, and listened to the music. John Henry kissed me and cuddled me and held my hand, and I have never been so happy, though even while he was kissing me, bold strumpets came up to him and begged for his favours – and when he turned them off, they requested a glass of wine, and drank to our health!

We visited the Rotunda to see the mirrors and paintings. A picture of the great fire, with flames leaping above the houses and people jumping from the roofs of houses, held me entranced, until John Henry dragged me away and made me look at the statues of famous people. He was so clever, he knew all their names. He was half Malayan, he told me, and that was why he was so handsome! Then we danced jigs and ended up in the early morning too tired to walk home.

One evening we visited the Haymarket Theatre, where we saw a play about Omar, the south Sea Islander who was brought to England and made famous. It cost three shillings each to sit in the pit, so we took seats in the gallery at one shilling. We sat next to apprentices who spent the performance throwing rotten oranges at the actors, who they did not think spoke loud enough. The apprentices complained they were paying good money for hearing nothing. Several young gentlemen in the pit banged with their sticks upon the rails whenever anything amused them or they were tired of it – it was hard to know which. The noise was very great, and the actors became hoarse. Omar himself was played by a very tall man with a blacked face, and he strode onto the stage in fantastic coloured clothes, with feathers in his hair. He spoke the oddest words. No one could understand him. The actors asked him to repeat his words, and tried to teach him English. So too, did the audience, and we were all shouting and correcting him, taking part in the play as though we were on the stage. One little actress could barely speak her lines, she was so frightened. The more she squeaked, the more she was pelted with rotten oranges.

When the play ended the audience yelled for more, and when the actors came to bow, half the audience cheered and half the audience booed and threw more oranges. It was an exciting performance, and I loved it.

My buying of fish suffered. Mrs Hillier did not approve of John Henry. She said sailors were all alike, in love one minute and off the next, and I would be mad to take him to my heart. She called me daft, moonstruck, a blockhead, and finally several choice names I will not repeat. She pointed out I did not know John Henry, he could be married, with several children. 'He says he is free,' she scolded me, 'but where is the proof of it?' She was furious that I had lost interest in her business, for she had found me useful. I was now easy to cheat, for I was starry eyed and in love. In the Dutch eel boats they mixed dead eels with live ones, and dead codfish were blown up with air to double them in size – and I never noticed these tricks, now that I had John Henry.

John Henry would find me in the market wherever I was, and lift me in the air and kiss me so heartily all the porters would cheer. It was difficult to hear each other over the noise of the market, the clattering of hooves, hackney carriages drawling over the cobbles, waggons grating and rumbling, cabriolets flying past, knocking over anyone in their way, and under it all the yelps of dogs kicked off the piles of fish, and cries of children mingling with the vendors bawling out, at the tops of their voices, 'Haaaaaaandsome Cod! The Best in the Market!' 'Sprats! Buy my fat sprats!' 'EELS! Juicy live eels!' 'Bloaters! Yarmouth Bloaters! Come and buy my bloaters, cheap for you!' 'OYSTERS! As many as you can eat for a penny!' And over it all the cry of the newsvendor, 'There's food for the belly and clothes for the back but I sell Food for the mind!'

But I DID hear John Henry say, as he squeezed my waist and hugged me so hard I dropped my basket, 'Come Mary, let's be married! We've waited too long as it is!'

Mrs Hillier was angry when I informed her I was off to be married. She stared at me, open mouthed. I think she hoped John Henry would leave me, or be press-ganged back onto a ship.

'I'd wish you luck,' she said, 'but I thought better of you Mary. You're a great gawping fool, lass. Can't you see he's not to be trusted? Now do you stay with me, deary, forget him,' she wheedled me. 'He's not worth your while, not a clever lass like you – he'll be nought but trouble, you mark my words.'

I didn't listen.

John Henry bought me a ring, I packed my few things in my trunk, and left.

We were married by a Romish Priest in a small dark room in a house in the Whitechapel Road. John Henry did not think Marriage in a Church necessary. I could barely see the Priest, a nervous, squinting old man with trembling hands, smelling of drink, for the tears of happiness rolling down my face. John Henry kissed my tears away and squeezed my waist, telling me I was his pretty duckling, his pet, so why was I crying so?

We did not tell my parents. They would not have ventured to London and my mother had not been in good health for some time.

We took lodgings and stopped a month in London. I delighted in being a married woman and John Henry lived for the pleasure he took in me. He began to teach me the Malayan language, as he had promised, and amused himself drawing signs for me to copy. He would tease me, pretending to sigh and praise my beauty, speaking in a strange language and looking at me with great sheep's eyes. Then, when I blushed, laughing, he told me I had not understood him, he had been comparing my looks to those of a pickled herring, and my eyes to that of a codfish! When I attempted to learn Malayan he called me a parrot, a pretty poll, 'but more of a squawking fowl with a tail feather pulled out'.

All we possessed in the world was a bed stuffed with straw, a table, and a chair with three legs, but I have never been so happy.

John Henry was spending his money fast, and soon he began to look for work. We went to Kingston, where we had lodgings. From thence we travelled all round Brighton, and from there to Battle. At Battle John Henry gave me some money to take me to London, for he was proceeding to Dover, and from thence to Calais. He promised to write and send for me.

He never did.

It is too painful for me to dwell on my marriage. I do not know what became of John Henry. He could have been taken by the Press Gang. Maybe he left me because I told him I was expecting a child as he had said he did not wish to be tied to a family. I had done everything I could to prevent conception, but the Lord thought otherwise.

I returned to London and found service at Mrs Clark's, the Crab Tree,

Tottenham Court Road. Mrs Clark was happy to employ me until I was taken in labour, for her second chambermaid had left the previous week, eloping with a soldier.

Mrs Clark was a little, nervous woman with grey hair that fell into her eyes, and a yellow skin, much lined. The dark circles under her eyes were evidence of the sleepless nights she suffered.

We were a large company of servants. Three ostlers, two waiters, a couple of yard boys, myself, the chambermaid and the cook completed the household.

Stage coaches left from our yard, and we had stabling for ten horses. Hackney coaches drew up in the Tottenham Court Road outside. When the coach arrived we ran from the Crab Tree to help travellers alight and collect custom. As the steps fell with a clacketty clack and the dozen or more passengers on the roof, hemmed in by baskets, boxes, trunks, cages of fowls and even pigs, tried to alight, the ostlers and yard boys waited to help them down. Many a young woman squeaked with surprise as she clambered down from the roof – the ostlers and yard boys were free with their hands. The inside passengers were often numb with sitting in cramped positions and the air filled with cries of 'Take care sir, you'll fall sir.' 'Can I carry your bags?' 'Comfortable bed for the night, Ma'am?' 'Mind the step, sir.' 'Clean, good linen.' 'No bugs, I assure you.' 'Best of vittles, sir, good wine too.' 'Like a nosegay for the pretty girl, sir?' 'I hope you'll please to remember a poor boy.' 'Ah, caught you, sir, thought you'd tumble in the mud,' and, if the passenger wished to proceed, 'Want a coach, sir?' 'Here's a carriage, sir.' 'Coachman, stop at once!' 'Coach to the city?' 'This way, this way, clear the road for the lady and gentleman!' We could collect good vails [tips] if we helped noisily enough. It amused me to be part of the hubbub. 'Hold my arm, sir, I'll escort you to the fire.' 'Ma'am, I'll carry that dog for you, you don't wish it to splash you with mud.' I saw to it that the travellers were settled at the inn, if they wished for a bed for the night. I cried out for the chambermaid to light fires in the bedrooms and air beds, and sent a yard boy to tell the cook how many there would be for breakfast or dinner. After that I helped at table.

I had an hour each day to please myself and it amused me to walk up and down the Tottenham Court Road, which was haunted by strange characters. It was not a pleasant road. There was an open ditch running down one side, and behind it the brickworks. Hogs wallowed in the mud of the gutter and dogs fought over scraps. The smell of rotting vegetation was strong, for there were large piles of household waste. My favourite character was a strange man on a white pony, which he had painted with purple spots to match his dyed beard. He wore a peculiar black hat and black frock coat. He sold bottles of medicine, and pulled teeth, so fast that the tooth was out before the patient had opened his mouth. So it was said. He had a hooting manner of calling his trade, which attracted a great deal of attention.

Mr Shooter, the rat man, lived at the King John's Palace Public House, near the windmill, and walked everywhere covered in rats. While walking he fed them with sops from his mug of porter, and called them by name. They crept over his hands and shoulders and nestled in his hair. I stopped to speak to him several times.

'This is Peg,' he told me, holding a grey rat up for inspection, 'she lost a tail in a fight, see the stump – poor Peg can't balance now.' Indeed Peg had a curious manner of running up his arm. 'And here is Nelly, she had a litter recently in my HAT, if you please, I could not wear it, and caught a cold in the head. Here's Sam. He's the biggest; look at his ragged ears. Talk to me, Sam.' At the command a big black rat crept up his shoulders and stood on hind legs by his ear, appearing, by the twitching of his whiskers, to be communicating. 'O,' the rat man told me, 'Sam is in trouble. His wife has left him for a gentleman from the sewers.' I found this comical. He thanked me with the utmost politeness, as though I were a Duchess, for being interested in his rats.

After I had been at the Crab Tree several weeks, great excitement was caused in the neighbourhood by the discovery of the body of a sailor found floating in the soil pits in Charlotte Street. His relatives had thrown him there when he returned home on leave and had the misfortune to die of fever at their house. They explained he had left no money with which to be buried, and the pauper's holes were full. The open soil pit was a convenient way of disposing of the body.

Mrs Clark was very upset by this. She went to see the body, and told me the story four times in the space of an hour. I think she thought Mr Clark might dispose of her in this way if he killed her in a drunken fit.

Mr Clark was a most unpleasant man. Gross and lecherous, he had seduced many of the maids at the Crab Tree, turning them out of the house with the utmost indifference when it was found they were expecting a child. Mrs Clark wept as she told me this. She had pleaded with him in vain to send them away with enough money to keep them for several months, but he refused. She had been eager to employ me, she said, because I was already big with child, and Mr Clark had no feelings for women already pregnant. 'If I had had children,' Mrs Clark told me, her face wistful, 'it might have been different. I could not have them, Mary, and so it is largely due to me that Mr Clark has become so nasty.' I tried to tell her that this was not so, but she would not listen to me.

Mr Clark was a bullying sort of man, large, with a face covered in blotches. He spent most of his days in the basement, at the cockfighting pit, a pot of ale in his hand and money stuffed into his pocket. If he won, he would be good humoured. If he lost, he came howling upstairs, a stubble of grey beard on his chin, reeking of ale and pissing himself in his fury. When he passed out, one of the men would put him to bed in his boots.

Though I was used to lewdness and rough ways, Mr Clark could make me blush for shame. His hands seemed everywhere, huge, red hands with bitten nails. He frightened me very much. His bulk was so great he could not sit on a bench, but sprawled. If we paused in our work, he yelled at us. If, by mistake, we came too near, he lashed out at us, then told us he had been provoked. It amused him mightily to see us frightened. Sometimes he tumbled to the floor, drunk, and lay there, bellowing at us and threatening us with dreadful tortures, if we did not pick him up.

Mrs Clark loved him still. When he taunted her for her refined ways, and jeered at her for being so weak, she excused him on the ground of disappointment in life. 'He called me a rose, once,' she told me, 'is that not romantic? Has anyone called YOU a rose?' I had to confess they had not. I could not imagine Mr Clark calling *her* a rose, either. 'A rosebud,' mused Mrs Clark, 'waiting to be gathered.' This made me laugh. Mrs Clark looked wistful, for I was making fun of her memories, so I said I had recollected something and laughed at that, and she looked happier.

'Mr Clark is drinking so much it is making him rude and violent,' she told me. 'We are running into debt. It may be the debtor's prison for us, and O,' she shuddered, 'I shall die if ever I set foot in such a place!'

A YOUNG DOCTOR OF 1751

'Dr. Urquart at the entry changes his peruke for a tie wig and puts on a short coat as his full-skirted one would brush the walls and sweep from them the lice and other insects which infect them. The wards at first sight rather curious; the beds of moderate width and containing not more than three or four patients, but these placed the feet of one to the head of another so that each receives not the tainted effluvium of their respective complaints. In the infants' wards there were of course any from six to eight in one bed. Pregnant women have their own ward to which they are taken when the pains seize them . . . Those in the earlier stages are frequently put with those about to die so that comfort is had by both. The air is rather foul . . . since the windows cannot be allowed to open. For the safety of those that minister to them it is customary for them to carry some prophylactic which can be held to the nostrils . . . as a rule a sponge soaked in vinegar . . . '

Michael Brander, *The Georgian Gentleman* (Saxon House 1973)

CHAPTER EIGHTEEN

My Son is Born

When my pains began I did not think it was the child coming. It was almost dark. I was serving supper in the parlour of the Crab Tree. The pain was so great I dropped the dish of boiled potatoes on the table and ran back to the kitchen, crying out I had been poisoned, I had eaten something bad, I was dying. The company in the parlour were upset by my odd behaviour and began to question the food, but Mrs Clark laughed at me, telling me the child was coming, the folk in the parlour had nothing to fear, it meant I was near my time. She told me to hurry and get to the hospital, because they did not have a bed at the Crab Tree for a confinement. If I was to be ill, who would look after me?

'What ails the wench?' cried Mr Clark, and Mrs Clark, hurrying to get my cloak and bonnet, assured him I was as well as could be, but the baby was coming.

Mrs Clark helped me into the road, stopped a hackney coach, and had me inside before I knew what was happening. She pressed four pence into the coachman's hand and told him to take me to the City Road Lying-in Hospital. I sat in the coach, pressing my hands against my stomach, praying that the child would not arrive too soon. We rattled and jolted over every rut in the road, splashing mud everywhere, the carriage swaying from side to side with the speed, the horse whipped into a frenzy, pursued by yapping mongrels and street boys, the whole business so horrid I did not know whether to laugh or cry.

'Has it come yet?' called the coachman, peering around him to see me, as though afraid to look, 'Do not let it come yet! I cannot bear the sight of blood, I do not wish to be a midwife, my wife has no children. Hold onto the child, I beg of you!'

The hospital stood on the corner of City Road and Old Street, some miles away. When we reached it the door was locked. My coachman hammered and shouted, while I sat in the carriage and prayed. My pains were coming regularly and I did not want to move.

Finally the door opened. I was assisted into a long room filled with beds, the floor strewn with sawdust and a chamber pot under each bed. The room was crowded with women, each bed having one, and in some cases two, occupants. The Matron, Mrs Newby, came to see me, bringing with her several pupil midwives, one of whom helped to deliver me. The birth was easier than I feared, but the child so tiny and delicate looking I thought he was dead. One of the pupil midwives held him by his feet and slapped him, and he cried. Before they wrapped him in swaddling bands they showed him to me, and he was so like my own dear John Henry I began to cry, for I never thought to see his father again. They placed him beside me on the wooden cot and we slept, despite the noise.

When I woke again it was morning, and I had a fever. I could not believe I had given birth to so strange a creature. He looked so wise, so old. He opened his eyes, and they were blue, as blue as my sailor husband's.

Later a nurse came and asked me if I had my marriage contract. She told me they had allowed me in because I was far gone in labour, but the practice was to admit only married women, and that on receipt of a marriage contract.

'I have none,' I told her. 'I do not know where it went. I am married, but he has left me.'

'O,' she replied, 'then the Committee must be informed. You will swear you have been married legally?' 'Yes,' I replied, 'I can state the time and place.' Then I began to sob, for I remembered the early days of our marriage, and how much John Henry had loved me.

They asked me to spell my name, and I told them Beckerstedt, but they could not spell it. The child was crying, and after some whispering they left me.

Later they told me they were relaxing the laws about admitting only married women. The war had made many widows, or killed sweethearts intending to marry, so that it was often impossible to produce a marriage certificate.

My room had forty beds in it, arranged along the two sides, with a central fireplace at the end. Sashed windows, which did not fit properly, let in the air. The room stank. The chamberpots overflowed regularly as there were not enough nurses to do the work of cleaning the ward. I was glad to have a small cot bed to myself, for the fever made it difficult to move.

I was visited by a lady from the Committee the morning after my child was born. 'I trust you are well?' she asked me, holding a pomander to her nose. 'I thank you, Ma'am, I am.' 'And the child is a fine boy?' She peered at little John Henry as though he were an insect. For I had decided to name him after my husband, to keep John Henry's memory alive. 'I thank you, yes, Ma'am.'

I found it difficult to answer her with the right amount of humility, lying in bed, but I bobbed my head in such a way I hoped it looked respectful. 'Good,' she said, 'you have much to be grateful for. This charity provides you with shelter, food, and help. It enables you to give birth with the best care and medical attention. You must thank God for the comfort and luxury in which you find yourself.' She admonished me on my morals and set out the behaviour of a practising Christian, as though I was not one. She did not seem to believe I had been married. 'The hospital' she concluded, before handing me a tract on Christian Principles, 'is not for the maintenance of the indigent, the liar, or the thief. Nor is it a place for idleness.'

'I am none of these things.' I cried out, indignation causing me to rise up in the bed, ill as I was, 'I am here because my husband could not find work, and went abroad, and did not send money back for us.'

Little John Henry began to bawl and she put her hands over her ears and drifted away. She was wearing a military bonnet with plumes and they vibrated as though agitated. I also observed a redness about her neck and ears.

I do not think she complained of my pertness, for no one came to scold me for answering back.

The Rev. Joseph Cookson appeared later the same day. He was a gentle, sad man, and did not lecture us. He baptised children that were dying, and gave communion to any of the mothers the nurses thought were in danger. The living, or those that could walk, went to chapel to be churched on Sundays. Prayers were stuck up on a pasteboard beside each bed and we prayed together night and morning in the wards. The women had to attend chapel every day, and every woman who had given birth was expected to give public thanks for safe delivery, whether or not her child had lived.

I stayed in the hospital a week. We ate well, and I grew strong rapidly. We had meat every day, roasted on Sundays, Tuesdays and Thursdays, and boiled on Mondays, Fridays and Saturdays. On the last day it was made into a broth for those who were too ill to chew.

Dorcas, a pupil midwife, who had trained for three months and was now able to deliver children without any help, took a liking to me. She came and gossiped when she was not busy. She told me there were twelve salaried midwives who came to the hospital to learn the trade, also two salaried nurses, the Matron, and eighteen pupil nurses. When the patients were well enough to walk, they were expected to help in the wards, as in St George's Hospital.

Dorcas was red haired and talkative. I learned how Mrs Newby, the Matron, kept pigeons for eating, and how the Committee had met to discuss the suitability of the Matron keeping pigeons, for they came into the wards looking for food and left feathers and dirt everywhere. Mrs Newby was partial to pigeon's eggs and she informed the Committee that if the pigeons left, she left. The pigeons stayed.

But this was as nothing to the previous hall porter who had kept a hog in the back yard of the hospital, which upset the Committee even more than the pigeons. They discharged him, along with the hog. Weeks later they found him still living in the hospital, hiding in his wife's room. She was a nurse, and had her own feather bed and bolster, and he had hidden in her cupboard and only came out at night. The hog had been committed to a butcher. When the Committee finally forced him to leave, he went, taking with him the ebony clock from the hall, and was never seen again.

After several days in bed I was told I could get up and help with the nursing. We had to ask permission if we needed to rest. It was not hard work, but I was often tired.

The work was mainly cleaning, cooking, and helping in the apothecary's laboratory. This contained a large iron bath for cleaning hands and feet. The apothecary had twelve flannel garments in which we dressed the incoming patients while we inspected them and their clothes for vermin. Their clothes were often burnt, being full of insects. We also helped him issue candles for the wards, seven each ward in winter, and five in summer, extra only if there was an emergency operation. The apothecary, Dr William Babit, acted as assistant to the surgeon, carrying the black box of instruments behind the surgeon when he went to operate.

At night our ward had a gloomy, flickering look, as though we had all died and gone to hell. I began to feel haunted, having the child beside me. He was such a sickly baby, and not knowing what would become of us or how I could look after him if he lived, I would lie crying, thinking of my future.

I returned to Mrs Clark's when I was allowed to leave the hospital, to show her the child. She was pleased to see him, but said she could not use me as a servant now that I had a baby to care for. She advised me to take lodgings and get the child admitted to the Foundling Hospital. She paid me full wages, and with these I was able to find cheap lodgings for myself and John Henry in Charlotte Street, while I attempted to find out how I could get him admitted to the Foundling Hospital.

He was a feeble child, and did not suck well. He never seemed to settle. I thought it might be because he knew I could not keep him. Sometimes he would lie silently, his blue eyes staring at me. He rarely cried now. When my tears fell on his crumpled face he sneezed, and blinked.

I loved him so much.

I visited the Foundling Hospital, and told them I was unable to support

The Foundling Hospital where Mary Baker was forced to leave her infant son
British Library

the child, for his father had deserted me. I did not know where his father
had gone. I went to enquire on three Wednesdays, but each time the intake
was full. Each time they told me to try again the following Wednesday. There
were so many children being placed in the Foundling Hospital that they had
not room enough for all who wanted to go there. It was terrible to see women
leave the gates, sobbing as though broken-hearted, wringing their hands in
anguish; and the crying of the children was pitiable. Each child was sent out
to a wet nurse in the country almost as soon as it was settled, and it was seen
that it would live. Sometimes not enough wet nurses could be found. I
enquired, and found that the nurses were paid 2/6d a week to look after the
child, and if the child died, the committee never entrusted her with another.
At the end of the year, if the child lived, the nurse received ten shillings.
Until the child was four years of age, he would live in her cottage under the
observance of an inspector, and be visited by persons sent by the Committee.
Then he would be inoculated and sent to school, and when he grew of age,
he would be apprenticed to some trade.

I tried to think of some token to leave with John Henry, so that if I saw
him later, I would recognise him. I found a bent penny, and forced a hole
through it, and tied it to his wrist, kissing his little hand and telling him I
did not want to part with him, it was all I could do, for we would starve
together if I kept him.

John Henry was admitted into the Foundling Hospital on the last

Wednesday of the month. They gave me a guinea and told me I could keep him another month, by which time they would have found a wet nurse for him. After the month, they put my child in Foundling clothes, and I left him at the hospital.

How my heart ached.

Again I went into service, at Miss Ferret and Miss Field's Dancing Academy for Young Ladies, at Thornhaugh Street, near Russell Square.

Every Monday, between ten and four, I went to enquire after the health of my child.

As servant at the Academy, my uniform was a grey striped cotton dress, with plain white apron and a grey ribbon in my cap. After opening the door to the young ladies, I took their capes and pelisses and showed them to the salon, where the dancing master was waiting.

The young ladies prided themselves on the latest fashion and several comical incidents happened when I was there. They would appear in the doorway each day in a new garment in the hope of being the first with a fashion, longing to be greeted with exclamations of envy. A lady arrived one day in pantaloons that hung below her muslin frock. Miss Ferret told her her drawers were too long for a lady of her age. 'My Mama approves,' the girl replied, 'and the Princess Charlotte wears them, and mine are bordered with Brussels lace like hers, so I must be in fashion.' Miss Ferret did not argue. The Mama in question was titled. Later Miss Ffinch, who had very little bosom, arrived with the latest thing from Paris – a false bosom made of wax! This began to soften in the heat of dancing and I was called upon to cool her with cold compresses. The Misses Avery both fainted while dancing, and Miss Ferret feared the dancing master had been too complimentary, but when I assisted them outside I found that, though they appeared to be wearing nothing under their white muslin dresses, they were laced into the very tightest of corsets. They informed me, with pride, that it was the latest thing and quite the rage. The name for it was the Divorce Corset, for it separated one bosom from another.

Miss Ferret played on the harpsichord and Miss Fields, I discovered later, though in charge of the household, was a secret tippler of gin.

I trembled at the sight of Miss Ferret. She had a long pinched face, purplish in hue, which went a deep mauve colour when she was angry. She dressed in dark grey with a large silver cross at her throat. She would take the cross in her large hands, kiss it, then become abusive. It was as though her religion supported her anger.

Miss Fields was round and untidy, with her cap always a little sideways, for she scratched her wig, loosening the cap strings. Her mouth was a little round O which pursed in astonishment at anything Miss Ferret told her she had not done. Sometimes she trembled so much I had to lead her to a chair and sit her down and fan her.

'Mary, leave us!' Miss Ferret would say. Before I had time to leave the room, Miss Ferret's cold voice would begin,

'Matilda, why have you not . . . '

'Matilda, I thought I told you . . . '

'Matilda, it is quite disgraceful the way you . . . '

'How can anyone be expected to behave if . . . '

'You look quite ridiculous in that colour . . . '

'How can I be expected to run a select Academy when you . . . '

'Do you realise . . . ' and then a list of things, ending with the plea to set her cap straight, stop looking so stupid, and wipe that silly look off her face.

Miss Fields would sit upright in her chair, her cheeks crumpled and tears glistening in her eyes. If they dared to roll down her cheeks, Miss Ferret would pounce, like a cat upon a rat, and berate Miss Fields for a muddleheaded, incompetent bungler, and now this . . .

Tears! As if living with one so lacking in any social breeding, finesse, distinction, quality, was not enough! She had to cry like a . . . like a . . . servant girl!

I was fond of Miss Fields. At times she would come and find me, and in a hesitant, whispering voice tell me the things Miss Ferret had said to her, begging to be comforted and told they were not true. 'She has threatened to throw me out,' she would say, tears rolling down her cheeks.

I attempted to please her. Sometimes I picked bunches of wild flowers and left them on her bedside table, but this offended Miss Ferret and made her angrier than ever with Miss Fields.

One day I discovered Miss Fields scrabbling at the bottom of a box of blankets. When she heard my steps she let the lid fall with such a clatter it terrified us both. 'O Mary,' she said, her hand upon her bosom, 'I shall faint. Do not tell my sister. Please, please, do not tell my sister what you have seen. She would be so angry. I beg you, say nothing. How long have you been there, watching me: Did you see me take a little something from the chest? It is medicine I have for my cough. My chest is troublesome . . . ' and her head shook, while her eyes appealed to me to be sympathetic.

'But I saw nothing,' I told her. 'I heard the lid drop, that is all.'

'Then I need not have told you my little secret,' and Miss Fields' face flushed, and she became petulant. 'You would not have known,' she added. 'I am discreet, so very discreet,' and she stamped her foot and pouted like a child.

Later I found her weeping in a corner. 'My sister is not kind to me,' she sobbed. 'I would never do this if I was left alone, and not shouted at, and cursed. I am such a clumsy creature, but I become clumsier if I am found fault with. I cannot bear being scorned.' I comforted her as best I could.

One morning Miss Ferret discovered Miss Fields' hoard of gin, and there was much noise and shouting. Miss Fields held her apron over her face, not seeing where she walked for the greater part of the day. Snuffles came from behind the cloth, and little cries of pain. I felt sorry for her.

Miss Ferret turned on me. I was deceitful, she told me, wicked. I had lied by default. I had known of Miss Fields' weakness. Not a word. Miss Fields had confessed. Why had I not told her, Miss Ferret, of this? Such a sneaking, brazen hussy could not be allowed to stay in her house. I would have to go.

Miss Fields pleaded for me. It was not possible to hear what she was saying, for the cloth muffled the words, but through the sniffs and moans and shakings it seemed as though she were begging my pardon and beseeching Miss Ferret to reconsider her decision.

'Go to your room, Matilda,' cried Miss Ferret.

I was sad to leave. My uniform was pretty, and the work was light. The food was good, for we had to impress the young ladies, and I ate after they had finished. There was a great deal left over, for they watched their figures.

I had enjoyed seeing the young ladies dance and I practised several of the movements in my attic room at night, humming to myself. It was with a heavy heart I gave Miss Ferret back my dress, bonnet and apron, and set off once more in search of employment.

That same day I went to enquire after the health of my child, and found that he was dead.

COACH TRAVEL

'About nine o clock last night a serious accident was occasioned by two rival coaches endeavouring to a priority of entering into Brighton . . .

The Phoenix and Dart coaches, on leaving London, passed each other on the road, and the former kept the advantage within a mile of this town, when, making the rising turn of the road, the Dart endeavoured to run by, and by some crossing manoeuvre the leaders got entangled. In the exertion to extricate them, the pole of the Phoenix was broke and it upset. Very fortunately the horses got disentangled and ran away, otherwise the consequences must have been dreadful. Mr Taylor, of the Golden Cross Inn in this town (Brighton) had a thigh broken, Mr Cawthorne, a wine merchant of London, had his arm dislocated and several passengers and the coachman were much bruised. In consequence of the horses of the Dart taking fright, they ran away with the carriage, which had the dicky knocked off, and threw two of the passengers into the road, which entirely prevented the coachman rendering assistance to the party . . .'

The Annual Register (October 1816)

CHAPTER NINETEEN

My Time with the Gypsies

I was in sore need of comfort and wanted to see my mother. I had enough money from my wages to take the next coach home, and at Nelson's General Coach and Waggon Office at the Bull Inn, Aldgate Street, I found an afternoon coach leaving for Exeter. I booked a place on the roof, for that was cheapest.

Waiting for the coach to leave I sat on a crate of oranges and drank hot ale. I had never travelled on a coach and had heard stories of people freezing to death on the roof, or being crushed as the coach overturned when racing another coach. I could not afford to travel inside, in the warmth.

The coachman confirmed my fears. He was trussed up in hay bands and comforters, a greatcoat so padded he walked like a headless chicken. His face was red and nearly as old as the coach, and his scanty hair was as decrepit as the harness on the horses. The horses were so gaunt and spavined I wondered they did not die at the first flick of the whip.

There were three of us on the roof. A farmer who had had his pocket picked in the Abbey, and would not speak, a market woman in a red flannel petticoat and red wool cloak, who clung to me as soon as the coach started, and a drunkard who vomited over the side at the first bend, and fell off the roof on the second. The last we saw of him he was shaking his fist after the coach and swearing horribly, vowing we were galloping off with his entire possessions.

I found the motion exciting, and it cheered me. It felt like flying. The jolts did not worry me, though the old woman cried out 'O Lord! Lord!' and crossed herself as she left the roof at each bump and came down again, it seemed, harder each time. The farmer chewed his pipe and muttered he hoped to live, for his best sow was in farrow and needed his attentions.

When I arrived in Witheridge my mother was sympathetic and my father treated me almost with respect, for I had grown so much and was well dressed. I stayed a week and three days. My mother then insisted on accompanying me, carrying my clothes, for me to go to another place. She did not find one for me, so we sent my box to Bristol by the waggon, to be left till called for, and I walked on, going towards Plymouth.

My mother had comforted me much, by telling me I must not grieve, John Henry would be better off in Heaven.

It was getting dark. I had eaten nothing for some time, and was cold and footsore, so when I saw some gypsies by the road I stopped. The sight of the fire, and the food cooking, made me faint with hunger. I approached the fire.

A voice called out, 'Peace, or not peace?' I answered, 'Peace. I am cold, and hungry. Can I join you?' 'Be welcome,' said the voice, 'sit down and share our food.'

By the light of the fire I saw a gathering of about twenty persons, the men on one side of the fire, the women on the other, with children running in between. The flickering light cast shadows on their faces, which turned with enquiry to see what I was like.

'Sit,' repeated the old gypsy. He was a fine looking man, with snow white hair and beard, and an air of command. I later found out that he was the Rom Baro, the Big Man as they called the Gypsy Elder.

They gave me tea. Several pigeons were roasting in the embers of the fire, with roots and herbs boiling in a pot. The smoke, and the smell of food, made my eyes water.

I sat among the women, beside a gypsy whose chin was so long it rested on her breast as she stirred the pot with a ladle. She was very large, dressed in sackcloth apron and leather sandals. I was scared, for she looked like a witch, and the gypsies were feared by everyone, for it was thought they had the Evil Eye. They cursed you, and could make the curse stick. I had known many in the village who blamed the gypsies for an ailing cow or a sick sheep, and they abducted children to sell, it was said. They were not Christians, but neither were they Pagans. I did not find our what religion they practised, but they had a dread of ghosts and were relieved to find out that I was not one. They were afraid of clinging and disembodied spirits in the camp and so burnt the belongings of anyone who died, even their tents.

There were four tents in this camp. They were one family, the Rom Baro, the Grandfather, being their chief. His wife, their children, grandchildren, and even great grandchildren, comprised the gathering.

The Rom Baro was a great teller of tales. After the meal they sang and danced, while I watched, and then the Rom Baro began on what seemed to be his nightly stories. He told us how he had been much persecuted in the olden days, and beaten, threatened with hanging, and put in prison, simply for being a gypsy, which was classed as a vagabond. But he had always escaped by some clever trick.

The family were entertainers. They lived by singing, dancing with a fiddle and drum, and acrobatics. In lean times they used fortune-telling and mended pots and pans to augment their fortunes.

The Rom Baro declared I would be useful to them as he thought I would be quick and learn their ways easily. So I stayed.

I went with the women of the family selling baskets and bunches of flowers and herbs. I even told fortunes, and found it amusing that people believed me whatever I told them. But I only told them pleasant things, for they gave me double the money if I said something they wished to hear. 'You have crossed water many times' – this was safe, for it could be a river or duck pond and need not necessarily be the sea. 'Your heart is intent on something you long for – which you have been unable to achieve until now – do not despair – good fortune will come your way when you least expect it . . . you will live long and be prosperous . . .'

What came as a surprise to me was the division between male and female in the gypsy camp. Gypsies have a dread of contamination from females. This is called Marimee. Taboos can be for people, objects, or parts of the human body. I shocked the gypsies by showing my legs to them. Only young girls were allowed to show their legs. After you became a woman long skirts had to be worn. To touch a man with your skirt was wrong, for it belonged to the lower part of your body.

I found all this most difficult and strange. Women took second place in everything.

The gypsies told me I could make my fortune, for I was clever as a fortune-teller, danced and sang well, and was as nimble as they were in my somersaults. I had picked up some of their language, and this was useful to them, for I could understand part of what they said, and name a few objects also.

I was with the gypsies three days, but I left because they wanted me to do something I was unable to do. They plotted to steal money they knew to be hidden under the floorboards in an old woman's cottage, and needed me to climb into the cottage to retrieve it. The men knew exactly under which floorboard, for they had watched through the window under the pretence of mending her cauldron. There was a grille in the cellar, and I, being the most agile and smallest, would be dropped through it when she was asleep.

I could not do this. My mother's warnings rang in my ears. I had always been honest and feared God and Hell Fire, so I said goodbye to the gypsies and wished them well.

They were, I think, quite sad to see me go.

After leaving the gypsies I went across country to Teignmouth, and from Teignmouth to Honiton, acting all the way the part of a foreigner, and begging at farm houses. I avoided gentlemen's houses, for fear I should be detected, and wore my bonnet to make me look respectable.

I had ten shillings with me, and got on the stage coach a few miles from Bristol. In Bristol I tried everywhere for lodgings, but could not find any. Meeting with a young woman called Eleanor Biggins, I was directed to Mrs Neale's lodging house.

Here I stayed nearly three weeks, looking for work. I did not pretend to be a foreigner, until one day, for a frolic, we dressed ourselves up, I in a turban wound about my head, and Eleanor in a shawl and earrings. We went out into the streets and five shillings was given to us. I spoke only my lingo, and Eleanor was dumb. We were taken for strangers, newly arrived from a boat.

I had already enquired at the Quay to see if any vessel was bound for America, and was told that shortly there would be two or three. One Captain told me he would take me for £5 if I could find the money. There were already many passengers going and the vessel would sail in fifteen days.

I decided the only way to obtain this money without the risk of being apprehended as a vagabond and sent to the House of Correction, would be to garb myself as a foreigner and beg, my strange clothes and strange language protecting me from the Law. There was no other way to obtain £5 honestly.

I left my box at Mrs Neale's, telling her I would return, pay my arrears of rent, and claim it from her in a few days.

I dressed myself in a black stuff dress with a frill round the neck, a black and red shawl round my shoulders, my bonnet on my head, stout sandals of brown leather on my feet and black stockings. In a bundle I carried some necessaries and a piece of soap.

On my way from Bristol I dug a hole in a field under a tree, and placed my clothes inside, marking the spot with a large stone.

I left Bristol going towards Lamplighter's Hall by Lord de Cliffords. The people at Lord de Cliffords, being alerted by one of the gardeners, wanted to take me in, but I said no, for I was frightened of being found out.

I was constantly stopped on the road by people asking me, 'Where are you from? Where are you going?' and when I answered in my lingo they were astonished. One gave me 1/- and another, a farmer, took me home to show me to his wife. They fed me on roast veal, greens and potatoes. They showed great interest in me and could not stop exclaiming at my language.

After supper the farmer insisted on accompanying me to Lord de Cliffords to meet the French cook. The farmer and his wife had discussed my lingo and had decided it was French.

On arrival at Lord de Cliffords I did not want to enter the house, though the servants entreated me, and a great crowd gathered until I was forcibly pulled and pushed into the kitchen.

The French cook was moustached and round. He made a great fuss of me, giving me drink and food, but I would not eat, having eaten already. He could not understand my speech, but happened to ask if I was Spanish. Without thinking I answered 'si'. At this one of the servants exclaimed that he knew a Spanish woman in Bristol and would take me to her immediately. I made signs that I must retrieve my bonnet, which they had taken from me when I arrived, and so I escaped down the passage and out of the door, and thence over the fields until I was sure I was out of sight.

By this time it was raining, and I did not want to sleep in the fields, for I would be dirty in the morning.

I knocked on the door of a labourer's cottage, and was admitted by the wife. She was friendly and offered to put me up in the loft for the night. I was settling down to sleep in the straw when I heard through the cracks in the floorboards the labourer's voice saying, 'Perhaps she is a rogue, or a disguised man, someone come to murder us!'

I could not sleep all night for laughing. I thought I should have died with laughing before the morning, as the woman was nearly in fits, through fear that I was a disguised robber.

In the morning, having had one cup of tea, I crossed the Marsh and went on to Passage Road. I met a man who said, 'it is a fine morning'. I answered him in my lingo. I still wore my bonnet, and not a turban.

He accompanied me to the village. 'What a pity it is for you to go on without knowing anyone or being understood,' he told me. By signs, he said he wanted me to go with him to a French governess at a gentleman's house nearby. This lady insisted I was Spanish, but gave me a letter addressed to Charles Harvey, the French Consul, in Queen Square, Bristol, who, she said, might understand me, as he spoke Spanish well.

Thanking them in my manner, I left them. It was a warm day and when I came to a public house with a bench before it, I sat down to rest. The owner and his wife, by signs, begged me to come in and refresh myself, so I did.

Scarcely had I sat down than the man I had met earlier, a wheelwright's son, joined me. He had a friend with him, and they offered me many different kinds of drink, all of which I refused. He then said, if I was a Spaniard, I must drink brandy. I would be very fond of it, as it was much drunk in Spain.

They brought me a decanter of brandy, but I made signs that I did not want any. Then they brought me decanters of whisky and rum, to see whether I liked either of them. I took a little rum, and filled it up with cold water, and ate some biscuits.

I continued on my journey, but the wheelwright's son insisted on accompanying me. He said he had made it his mission to discover from whence I came, and what my lingo was. He added he had been paid to do it, by the French governess. I could not be rid of him.

He seemed to have a great knowledge of Spain, for he informed me, when we met some cows, that women rode cows in Spain.

A second man soon joined us, and when I spoke to him in my lingo he said I did not come from Spain, but from Madrid Hill. Then he left us.

I could not rid myself of the wheelwright's son.

We called at a public house and ate some beef steaks for dinner. After this we continued on our way back to Bristol, where he wished me to meet a Spaniard living in Clifton.

I made signs that I wished to go to the French Consul in Queen Square, and showed him my letter addressed to Charles Harvey. When we reached the square he stopped to ask the way to the house and was so deep in discussion about me that neither of them noticed when I slipped away. I hid myself behind one of the barrels on the Quay, and though he searched most diligently for me, calling and shouting and peering into every crevice, setting the dogs barking and children jeering, yet I was so well hidden he could not discover me.

After a time he gave up the search, and when I was sure he was out of sight I ventured out from my hiding place. I enquired for lodgings for the night in Bristol.

The next morning I set out for Almondsbury.

About half way to Almondsbury I took off my bonnet and put on my handkerchief as a turban. This made people call me French. At a public house where I stopped, they give me beer. When I reached Almondsbury Hill, I went into a shoemaker's shop for lodgings, but they did not understand what I wanted, and put bread and butter in front of me. Then they showed me to a Mr Hill, who did not want anything to do with me, and he sent me away to the Rev. Mr Hunt, who was not at home.

I went in, saw a bed, and made signs that I wanted to sleep there.

Mrs Hunt was alarmed by my appearance, and sent me to the Overseer of the Poor, who offered me sixpence which I did not take, making signs that I only wanted lodgings for the night.

The Overseer took me to Mr Worrall.

The rest you know.

THE SEARCH FOR
THE 'TRUTH'

THE TRUTH ABOUT
MARY WILLCOCKS

'In her narrative to Mr Mortimer, having asserted that her parish was Witheridge in Devonshire, and that the name of her parents was WILCOX; Mrs W. before she proceeded further in rendering her any assistance, determined to ascertain how much of truth and what there was fiction, in the account Mary had given of herself, requested a "tradesman" to visit her parents in Devonshire; from the minutes which this gentleman took on that occasion, the following particulars are extracted.'

J.M. Gutch, *Caraboo* (Bristol 1817)

CHAPTER TWENTY

Captain Palmer Investigates

Letter from Captain Palmer, The Inn, Tiverton
to Mrs Worrall, Knole Park
June 18th 1817

Mrs Worrall, Madam,

I write as soon as I am able. I am honoured that you have entrusted such a delicate mission to my rough hands, and trust that I will make a good job of it. The roads have been execrable, chiefly holes and mud and where there is not mud, there is dust and stones. One horse was lamed and one cast a shoe. I fear that I am a bad companion in a coach, for I am plagued by pains in my leg and must needs take up more room than is usually offered.

These are but small troubles, Ma'am, when compared with your own. The imposture has been a blow to us all. How foolish I feel, remembering my labours. The hours I spent uncovering her story. She has been clever, I feel, but not wicked. Seeing her before my departure I could not, I own, bear her a grudge. She has given us much to remember. I felt young again as she capered and danced.

I write from the Inn at Tiverton, and have been to see Mr Dickins, the Vicar of Witheridge, who resides here.

He is an amiable man, who but recently retired from his Parish. He lives in a large stone house accompanied by six Persian cats, of whom he is very fond. His housekeeper informed me that they are so much part of his life that he will take them into his bedroom – nay – will even bid them sleep upon his bed! He greeted me cordially and we discussed a fondness for cats (which, I own, I only felt at this moment). I explained I had business of a delicate nature with him, but did not immediately explain the reason for my coming. We discussed many things while I pondered on how best to approach the subject of the Willcocks family. At length he invited me to

Caraboo.

A

NARRATIVE

OF A

SINGULAR IMPOSITION,

PRACTISED UPON THE BENEVOLENCE OF A LADY

RESIDING IN THE VICINITY OF THE CITY OF BRISTOL,

By a young Woman

OF THE NAME OF

MARY WILLCOCKS, *alias* BAKER, *alias* BAKERSTENDHT, *alias* CARABOO, PRINCESS OF JAVASU.

Illustrated with TWO PORTRAITS, engraved from Drawings by E. BIRD, Esq. R.A. and Mr. BRANWHITE.

QUI VULT DECIPI DECIPIATUR.

PRINTED BY J. M. GUTCH, 15, SMALL STREET, BRISTOL ;

AND PUBLISHED BY BALDWIN, CRADOCK AND JOY, PATERNOSTER ROW, LONDON.

Price 5s.

1817.

The title page of J.M. Gutch's Narrative, 1817 *British Library* dine. His housekeeper informed him the meal was on the table, and that an extra place was laid for me. We discovered many mutual friends in Bristol. It was a most pleasant occasion.

'Mr Dickins,' I asked him, 'are you familiar with the Willcocks family of Witheridge?'

'Indeed yes', he replied, 'I married Ellen and Tobias Willcocks.' He looked puzzled. 'Mr Dickins,' I said 'do you know of any strangeness in that family?'

'No,' he assured me, 'no, they are honest, hardworking people, fallen on hard times these last few years.'

At this I felt the news I had to give him was so strange I did not know how to express myself.

Seeing I was silent, Mr Dickins leant forward. 'Surely this is not the grave matter you wished to discuss with me?' he asked. 'They are quite unremarkable as a family. They have had eleven children, seven of whom died in infancy. The older children are sent as servants or farm labourers. They are a modest family, and much liked.'

'Do you remember a daughter, Mary?' He said that he did. 'A strong-willed girl,' was his verdict, 'something of a tomboy.'

At this I told him everything.

He was silent when I had finished, as though stunned. At last he burst out, 'Can this be true? I CANNOT believe it. You know for certain that it is Mary Willcocks of whom you speak?' His amazement was so great I began to doubt my own story. 'How could a girl, as uneducated as I know Mary Willcocks to be, have supported a part of such duplicity?'

I agreed with him. This was the fact that had astonished us all, on finding out the truth.

'I think,' I told him, 'she believed so deeply in her fantasy that it became reality to her. She would even speak in her lingo in her dreams, and when ill of the fever.'

'It is all most odd,' said Mr Dickins. 'Whence came the knowledge to play a Princess? How came she to know so much about the East?'

'I fear,' I replied, 'that we helped. I by showing her maps, and discussing the most obvious route she might have taken across the seas. Mrs Worrall and myself by discussing, in front of her, our ideas on her country and language. She could read, remember, she has a retentive memory and a clever brain.'

Mr Dickins shook his head. 'Is it possible that Mary Willcocks could dupe so many people, such fashionable people, for so long? You say it is so. You must know. But what of Mrs Worrall in all this? Is she deeply upset? Such a blow to her kindness must trouble her greatly.'

While speaking he was pacing the room, deeply troubled. I assured him,

Ma'am, that you had formed a deep attachment to Mary and that her affection for you was also great. He was full of praise for your generosity and Christianity, and devoutly wished there were more good Samaritans in the land with such charity in their hearts.

My letter must end here. I hope to catch the mail coach with this pacquet. Tomorrow I am to go to Witheridge to meet Mary's parents, and Mr Dickins has promised to accompany me. He fears a stranger arriving with this news could seriously alarm the Willcocks'. Mrs Willcocks is ailing, and Mr Willcocks' eyes have become troublesome, due to the close work he has done. They brought Mary up God-fearing and truthful, he assured me. The father is a strict disciplinarian, and never spared the rod. My fear is, this will be a terrible blow.

When next I write, I shall be in a position to give you a fuller account of Mary's character and past activities.

I remain, Madam
Yr. obedt. humble svt.
J.C.M. Palmer

Letter from Capt. J.C.M. Palmer, Witheridge, Devonshire
to Mrs Worrall, Knole Park
June 13th 1817

Mrs Worrall, Madam,

I trust you received my last letter and the news brought some comfort to you.

Today has stopped raining. Mr Dickins and I travelled by post chaise to Witheridge, the better to enjoy the scenery, and were caught in a downpour, in consequence of which I have had some trouble with my leg. We are, however, comfortably settled in the lodging house and this morning sent for Mr and Mrs Willcocks. Their house, Mr Dickins informs me, is unsuitable for such a meeting. Mr Dickins has been a most pleasant companion, and we agree well on most points. His text for next Sunday is 'We are but Strangers and Pilgrims through Life', which he thought apt.

We had scarce finished our Tea when Mr and Mrs Willcocks arrived. Both neatly dressed, but in clothes much patched and darned. They looked apprehensive at the sight of me, but brightened on observing Mr Dickins, who greeted them warmly. After some polite exchanges as to weather, children etc. Mr Dickins informed them I had something of import to tell them. They must not be alarmed, for there was nothing in it of law-breaking.

Mr Willcocks thought I had been sent to reprimand him. He has many troubles and began to tell me some of them, in so excitable a way, and with so many gestures, I began to see where Mary had inherited some of her talent. I was hard pressed to stop the flow. The gist of his argument is the enclosures. These, he says, have ruined him. They have driven him to paupery and ruined his business. Where before he had a horse, a cart, and a pig, now he has nowhere to pasture the horse and can no longer get to market without a vehicle to carry him. His business has fallen off as a result.

He became so flushed during the outburst that I feared he would do himself harm. There is more than a hint of temper in his face and obstinacy in the set of his lips. His complexion is ruddy on the cheeks, but of a sallow tone. It is possible to see traces of Mary's face in his, for his hair must once have been dark. It is now quite grey.

Mrs Willcocks has certain similarities to her daughter, though being past her youth, her skin is much wrinkled and her hair flecked with white. She stoops, and appears unwell (her cough is troublesome), but her manner has dignity. Her eyes are large, expressive and brown.

I interrupted Mr Willcocks with a request that he and Mrs Willcocks be seated, for I had a great deal to tell them. This stopped him in mid sentence. Mr Dickins added gently that it was not about himself and his wife that I came, but about some other matter entirely. Mr Willcocks begged pardon for so forgetting himself as to unburden his grievances.

So that you, Madam, may feel yourself present at this meeting, I have listed here my questions and their replies. I hope that this information gained from Mary's parents will help to our greater understanding of Mary.

Mr Willcocks here speaks.

'How many children have you?'

'Four. The eldest is a son about 32 years of age, then a daughter, Mary, and another son and daughter 14 and 9 years old.'

'Can I see your daughter Mary?'

'I cannot fetch her, for she has left us. I do not know where she is.'

'When did she leave you?'

'About eight years ago. We have seen her several times since, and she had a good position near here, but she left it.'

'Why did she leave?'

'I cannot tell why, unless it was on account of the strap. I beat her well with the strap, for she disobeyed me once, going with another girl to a fair at Exeter. I flogged her well about two years ago, for going contrary to my consent.'

'At what age did she begin employment?'

'At the age of sixteen she went into service with Mr and Mrs Moon of

Exeter, where she remained for upwards of two years, and then ran away to London.'

'How did you hear she ran away?'

'We heard of her running away from a girl who ran away with her, and grew tired of the journey and returned. Afterwards we learnt Mary was ill and a waggoner gave her a lift to London, and set her down at an Hospital, where she was a long time confined in a fever. On the day she was to be discharged, a gentleman, whose name was Mr Puttenden, was visiting a poor woman in the same ward, and being informed of Mary's forlorn and friendless situation, he enquired into particulars of her life. Mary gave him Mrs Moon's address and he told her, if Mrs Moon gave her a good character, he would find a place for her.'

'I see. Did Mrs Moon give Mary a good character?'

'Yes sir. Mrs Moon gave a good account of Mary. So Mr Puttenden took her to his own home. He procured a place for her soon after, with Mrs Mathews of Clapham Road place, where she continued for three years.'

'Did you hear from Mary in all this time?'

'Yes sir. We frequently heard from her at Clapham Road place. She sent us a pound bill. She was very happy and comfortable. When she wrote, she sent us money, whatever she could save. She was always much liked, wherever she lived.'

'She left Mrs Mathews after three years – why did she leave?'

'I do not know why she left. She came to Witheridge soon after, and stayed a little while at home. She then went into service with Mr Sandford, an Attorney of Exeter. She lived with him for some time, and left him with a good character. She then went back again to London, and Mr Puttenden having promised to befriend her again she applied to him, and he soon placed her in the service of Miss Fields, where she stayed a few months before quitting London and returning home.'

'How long ago was this?'

'About a fortnight before last Lady-Day.'

'Did you have the curiosity to make enquiries who Mr Puttenden was?'

'Yes sir. The son of a neighbour, a linen draper in London, went to find out. He is a highly respectable character, a Presbyterian Minister, much beloved in the neighbourhood.'

'Was Mary clever at school?'

'She went to a neighbourhood house to school, and she could read, though she could not write. Ann Baker who taught her, was unable to write also.'

'Mary can write now. Who taught her?'

'Mrs Mathews taught her to write. When she was at home she spent most of her time reading. Her head was always in a book. It was not good for her. I tried to stop it.'

'Did you hear of Mary being married?'

'Yes. When she returned to us from Miss Fields we knew she had been married. She wrote and told us so. She had a child four months old, who died before she left London.'

'Did you meet her husband?'

'No sir. We never saw her husband. She told us she had left him at Dover, and had come to take her leave of us, before she went to the Indies.'

'Did she say which Indies?'

'No. She did not tell us whether it was the East or West Indies.'

'And you have not seen her since?'

'No sir. She gave us some money, and bade us farewell. She took her leave, and we have not heard from her since.'

'Did you observe any difference in her behaviour, during her last visit?'

'She seemed very learned and well dressed. She could talk French very fast, and used to talk for two or three hours in a morning to her sister in bed.'

'How did you know it was French?'

'Because the folks in the village said it was so. But I think she was not always right in the head. Ever since she was fifteen years old, in consequence of the rheumatic fever which affected her head, I believe she was not right in her mind. At Spring and Autumn she is particularly uneasy, always wishing to go abroad.'

'Has she any other weakness?'

'No sir. She is not fond of tippling. She rarely drinks anything but water.'

I then told them why I had questioned them so closely about their family, and especially Mary.

Mr and Mrs Willcocks were much moved. They begged pardon for their daughter's misdoings and implored the lady of the house where she was staying (yourself, Madam) to forgive Mary, and endeavour to place her in some situation where she could maintain herself. They prayed God to bless you for your kindness to their daughter. They repeated many times that you were Mary's saviour and benefactor. They could not grasp the fact of Mary's duplicity and were so bewildered by it all, I do not think they fully understood what she had done.

They told me they had some letters from Mary, which I asked them to give to me.

I enclose the letters. They give some insight into the change in Mary during the years after she left home. You will, I hope, find them intriguing.

There is an allusion in one of the letters to a present sent by Mr and Mrs Willcocks to Mr Puttenden. This was three fat ducks and a pint of cream. I doubt if he knew how poor they were. They told me Mr Puttenden had saved Mary from ruin by his attention and advice.

This, Madam, must be the conclusion of my letter. I trust I have not wearied you, with the length of it. I know how eagerly you must await the results of my mission.

I am spending a week at Taunton among cousins. I fear they will wine and dine me until not a traveller's tale is left me and my wits are fuddled completely.

I am sending this pacquet by the evening mail coach, and trust it will reach you safely.

It is a comfort that all who knew Mary became fond of her, and in the situations where she worked she was known as honest, industrious and God fearing. We have heard no ill of Mary save that she is headstrong and restless. I will be delighted to carry on investigations should you so wish it. The exercise is doing my leg a power of Good and my curiosity is much aroused.

How little we shall ever know of such a girl!

I remain, Madam,
Your obdt. humble svt.
J.C.M. Palmer

Letter from Mary Willcocks
to Mr and Mrs Thomas Willcocks of Witheridge, Devonshire
London. July 1st 1816

My dear Father and Mother,

What apology to make I know not for my undutiful conduct for which I beg your forgiveness. I have been travelling abroad with a family this long day back, and have lately returned from the Continent. You have, I believe, heard that I was married, and have got a son about four months since, which we have called John Henry. I am going to Norwich with my husband, who is a native of that place, but I am not sure whether we shall remain there or not, but I will write to you every three months, and let you know every particular of our situation. Give my love to my brothers Henry and Thomas, and my sister, and let me know what trade you intend to bind Thomas to. I send you – as a small mark of my love and duty, and I shall send you in future, please God – half a crown a week; but it will answer as well to send it yearly.

I beg you will write to me directly, for fear I should happen to leave London before I receive your answer.

I conclude with my love to brothers and sister, and kind compliments to all friends.

Your ever dutiful daughter
Mary Willcocks

P.S. Direct for me to Mr Paddington, No. 20 Coppice Row, Clerkenwell, London.

My husband (Baker) whose christian name is the same as his son, sends his love and duty to you.

Letter from Elizabeth Flower
to Mr Thomas Willcocks, Witheridge, Devonshire
London. Jan 18th 1817

Dear Sir,

Being a friend and acquaintance of your daughter's, Mrs Baker, who was sent to France before Christmas with her husband, she left me a pound note to charge for you, which I now enclose. I should have sent it before according to her orders, but waited in hopes of receiving a letter from her, that I might be able to acquaint you of her safe conduct in France, but as I have not heard from her since, I judged it not wise to delay sending you this letter and its inclosure any longer.

I hope you have heard from her before now. I have a box of clothes belonging to her, also a check on the bank for £25 which she desired me to send to you in case of anything happening to her. I sent by Betsey Dinner, two gowns to her sister, before she went to France. I almost forgot to mention that her child died about a fortnight before she left London.

You will please to answer this by return of post, as I intend to write to her shortly.

I am Sir, with respect, your very humble Servant
Elizabeth Flower

Please to direct to me at No. 24, Wilmot Street, Brunswick Place, London.

Captain Palmer has been to visit Mr and Mrs Willcocks and spoken to Mr Dickins, the previous Vicar of Witheridge, who knew Mary when she was a child.

His letters are so unlike him! Not the blunt Captain Palmer I know in conversation, but a man almost verbose in his reports. I believe he is enjoying the detective work, for he reports whole conversations in the most novel way.

His letters are keeping my mind occupied while I wait for Mary's vessel to sail.

I hope I am beginning to understand Mary. She is a strange girl, but there is no harm in her. Her parents are honest, God-fearing, hard working people. Her exploits have been a great shock to them.

She is still the toast of Bath and Bristol.

She has quitted Knole (for indeed, how could I have asked her back here, after her duplicity became known?) She is staying in Bristol with Mr Mortimer, who is not easily cajoled by her wiles. His housekeeper, Mrs Dinner, takes good care of her and insists on accompanying her to St Thomas's where she is preached to and prayed for by the Rector and congregation. I hear the church is so besieged they are issuing tickets.

She shows little contrition for the part she has played. She seems to glory in her fame, however dubious it is. I confess I have no heart to wear my military bonnet again; it is so very striking, and I cannot bear to be stared at and pointed out. When life is delightful and full of interest the bonnet seemed the height of fashion – but now – no.

Public curiosity has increased, rather than diminished. The Earl of C–k came from Bath for the sole purpose of conversing with Mary. The Marquis of S–y requested the same indulgence! She is visited by people of all descriptions; physiognomists, craniologists, and Gypsies – all anxious to see Caraboo. This publicity will turn her head completely. Mr Mortimer informs me that he has hired two footmen of great height and width to guard his door and dissuade people from entering.

I had wished to place her with a pious family where she would be safe from such attentions, but Mr Mortimer persuaded me that he was the proper person to have care of her, for he knows her well.

The Rev. Dr Freeling told me yesterday that Mary has an impenetrable heart. I do not know what he means. When I appear she shows such gratitude and affection, running towards me like a Child, begging to be forgiven, and sometimes, forgetting the Play is over, falling on her knees at my feet, and attempting to kiss the hem of my dress, to the amusement of all who watch. Or she covers my hands with kisses, as though I were the only person in the world she cares for.

I have had so much time to think, and have felt so unhappy, and yet I cannot blame myself for being so taken in. She still exudes an air of – I do not know what it is – an air of regality – an air of power –

Mr Worrall is still in the Dumps about the Bank, and can offer me no sympathy. Indeed, yesterday he told me, 'the sooner we get rid of her, the better for us both.' I did not reply.

She is now dressed in clothes more befitting her station in life. I have had made for her a modest lavender striped gown with apron, fichu and bonnet. She looks most charming. I have paid her passage on the *Robert and Anne*. The Captain is a Mr Robertson, a stout, good hearted sailor, who swears he will look after her as if she were his own daughter.

The *Robert and Anne* has nearly completed her cargo. Captain Robertson is carrying a mixed cargo of goods including pig iron, mallets, glass bottles, tobacco pipes, woollens, carpeting, cheese, tripe, a bedstead, two fowling pieces and one chest of stationery, and among all this, Mary and several other passengers. They will sail once the bedstead arrives and the wind is favourable.

I have agreed with Captain Robertson to furnish Mary with clothes, money and food for the voyage, sufficient to support her till she can find service in Philadelphia. I have found three young females among the passengers who are going as teachers to a Moravian establishment in Philadelphia. I have prevailed upon them to offer her their protection during the voyage, to see that she comes to no harm. I told them to offer Mary pecuniary assistance if they approve of her conduct during the voyage.

We have entered her name as Mary Burgess, for now the names 'Willcocks' and 'Baker' are too well known. She MUST travel incognito, for I fear she is become conceited, and might play her part to the end.

I must remember to write to Captain Palmer and beg him to continue his detection work. I wish to follow up every clue to Mary's past life as she has confessed to it. It will occupy my mind *after* she has sailed, too, for I will feel so very strange without her after all these weeks.

Letter from Mrs Worrall of Knole Park
to Jane Worsthorn of Stony Easton Lodge
June 18th 1817

Dear Jane,

My heart is so full, I MUST write to you. Mary Willcocks sailed today to Philadelphia. Some day, Jane, we may look back and laugh at this, but now my eyes are full of tears, for O Jane, I was so fond of her! She made life magical for a time. You will berate me for being sentimental, I know.

A note has arrived from the ship. The *Robert and Anne* was laying in Kingroad on the Severn, and our tower can be seen from the river. One of the Moravian ladies has written that Mary's eyes have been full of tears every time she looked up and saw the house. She has waved at the tower in the hope that I am looking from my window, and can see her. I waved back just now, but the vessel has gone. The river is empty.

Mary wrote me these verses before she left and sent them with the note. Do you think they are her own?

> 'Friendship thou charmer of the mind
> thou sweet deluding ill
> the brightest moments mortals find
> and sharpest pains can feel.
> Fate has divided all our shares
> of pleasures and of pain
> in love and friendship all the cares
> are mixed, and join again.'

I can write no more.

Affect.
E.W.

Letter from Jane Worsthorn of Stony Easton Lodge
to Mrs Worrall of Knole Park
June 18th 1817, p.m.

Dearest C.

OF COURSE she cared for you.

You silly goose, she was devoted to you. How could she not be? You gave her everything she wanted from life and made her fantasies come true.

Affect.

Jane

CHAPTER TWENTY-ONE

An Enigma to the End

Letter from Captain Palmer, 5 Market Street, London
to Mrs Worrall, Knole Park
July 1st 1817

Mrs Worrall, Madam,

London is a most noisome and brutal place, swarming with flies, brigands, dirty rascals who rob you as soon as look at you, and stench. The stench, Madam, is past belief! But as you were so kind as to request me to continue my work of detection, I shall stay here until it is finished. My leg is passable, and I hobble from coach to hackney coach, knowing that I am being of help to you, Ma'am, who deserve all the goodwill in the world after your generosity and kindness to that girl.

But to business.

I found Mr Puttenden, a Dissenting Clergyman, at No. 29 Coppice Row, Spitalfields. He has a neat, tidy house, and a maidservant who opened the door and led me to the parlour, where Mr Puttenden presently appeared. He is large but of an amiable disposition, confessing to twinges of gout in his right leg, at which we discussed our various infirmities and thus cemented a bond of friendship between us. He confirmed Mary's story, in that he took her out of the Hospital and procured for her a place at Mrs Mathews. He also got her child into the Foundling Hospital, and his daughter (whom I did not see) was the first to hear that it was dead when she went to enquire after it.

Mary told him that the child's father was the MASTER of a Family whose service she had been in, in the country. She had been seduced and thereafter left his employment.

This throws a new light upon the matter, does it not?

Mr Puttenden regretted that twelve months ago he lost sight of Mary. He and his family always took a great interest in her, and she came to him whenever she was in need of help.

I told him the story of Caraboo and how Mary had deceived us all.

He was astonished.

'I did not think there was very much harm in her,' he told me. 'She was always so odd and eccentric that I could fill a volume with her doings if I had time. She would tell such stories as would make a person's hair stand on end.'

He then paused, and looked at me, and added, 'Many times I tried to bring her to reason, but she always swore that what she said was true.'

I told him the story of her staying out all night, and this being the reason she had left Mrs Mathews' place. She was afraid he would scold her when she returned in the morning, for he had waited up for her.

'I do not remember a word of it,' he said. 'Mary left Mrs Mathews without warning. We never did understand the reason for her going. She did not give it. Mrs Mathews was much hurt at the time, for she had done a great deal for Mary.'

I then asked him if Miss Puttenden was about. He answered no, she was out with her Aunt for the day, but he would ask her to write to me when she returned.

The day after my enquiry I received a letter by messenger from Miss Puttenden, who wrote:

Hon. Sir.

Agreeable to yr. request, I write to you what further information I have respecting Mary Willcocks. We suppose, Sir, she had her lying-in in February 1816, as to the Place where – her accounts were contradictory. To one she said, the child was born on the road to London; to another she said, that she had had her lying-in at the Westminster Lying-in Hospital. The child was taken to the Foundling the 6th day of June 1816, and we suppose it was baptized there, and we think it lived about two months after, or a little more.

We have not seen her, I believe, since last Xmas.

The family she lived with in Islington was a Mrs Starling, the corner of Norfolk Street, near the Thatched House, the lower part of Islington.

The pay she received for the child was from Lambeth Workhouse. It is likely they can give some account of the father, as in this, as in many other matters, her accounts varied. To some she said it was her Master, a French gentleman at Exeter. To others, it was a young gentleman under his care. And to yet others that it was a foreign sailor who disappeared one night. At the Foundling the father was entered in the book as a labouring man who worked at her Master's. She said his name was Baker.

I think, Sir, you have the address of Mrs Mathews, No. 1 Clapham Road Place, where she was soon after we had first knowledge of her.

I wish, Sir, we could give you more information, and sincerely pray, notwithstanding her past conduct, which displays great Wickedness, that God may give her Grace to repent, and that in some future day we may hear of her being a Bright and Shining Character, one that truly fears God and departs from all iniquity.

I am, dear Sir, your very
humble servant,
P. Puttenden
29 Coppice Row
Spitalfields

This is as far as I have got. I trust it will be of interest. I send this letter post haste by the night mail coach.

I remain, Madam,
Yr obedt. humble svt.
J.C.M. Palmer

*Letter from Captain Palmer
to Mrs Worrall, Knole Park
July 3rd 1817*

Mrs Worrall, Madam,

You will no doubt be waiting with great interest for the results of my visit to London. I write to tell you of my further enquiries. I will be as brief as the circumstances allow.

Though some of Mary's employers have moved, I have so far been able to trace their whereabouts, and am rapidly gaining a much better grasp of Mary's character and doings. So far there have been no adverse criticisms of her, which has pleased me as much as I am sure it will please you.

Today I enquired at the Crab Tree Public House, in the Tottenham Court Road. It lies in a poor neighbourhood, but both Mr and Mrs Clark seemed decent enough folk though scraping about for a living. Mrs Clark remembered Mary very well, and confirmed that she had lived there six months, staying until she was taken in labour.

I enquired what happened then?

Mrs Clark told me that a hackney coach stopped for her, and the coachman had been most solicitous, but they did not know where he had taken her.

I then asked, would any of the hackney coachmen remember Mary? She told me there were one or two who regularly worked in the Tottenham Court Road, and pointed them out to me.

By the greatest coincidence, on quitting Mrs Clark I found, on addressing the nearest coachman, a burly fellow with a scarf wound many times round his throat although it was a warm day (on closer inspection I saw he had a disfigurement he was attempting to cover), that he had been the very man to stop for Mary when she ran from the Crab Tree Public House. Could he remember, I enquired, a girl, big with child, a year or so back, who had been servant at the Crab Tree Public House?

Indeed he could, he informed me, he remembered Mary well, and he described her to me in great detail. She had been printed on his mind for her curious manner of proceeding. Though in pain she would not be driven to hospital, and insisted he set her down on the road, a mile of so from the Crab Tree, among the brick kilns. Being anxious about her state he watched her, to see where she was going. She eluded him and disappeared among the trees, and although he followed her a little way on foot, it was to no avail.

Mrs Clark says that though Mary called at the Crab Tree afterwards, with the child in her arms, they could never find out where she lay-in.

I asked her, was Mary peculiar in any way? She answered me, no, during the six months Mary was with her she conducted herself with the utmost propriety, she was particularly modest in her behaviour, and one of the most cleanly, regular good servants they had ever had. She passed by the name of Hannah, but in her Bible, which she used to read on Sunday, the name of Mary Baker was written.

She told Mrs Clark her husband was dead, and that he died of the fever, but they thought she had never been married. They were very partial to her. She scarcely ever went out, but told such odd, unaccountable tales that she became proverbial among them for the marvellous. They were stories, however, and never harmed anybody. She seemed to tell them for the love of telling something extraordinary.

I thanked Mrs Clark for her time, and she was most interested in all that had happened to Mary since she left the Crab Tree, and wished me to send her good wishes to you, Ma'am, for all you did for Mary. Indeed, Mary has told us some odd tales about the Clarks, which is surprising for rarely have I met such a well mannered couple.

I am keeping several days investigation together, to be sent you in one pacquet, for ease of delivery. I go tomorrow to Miss Ferret and Miss Fields.

July 4th 1817

I have been today to see Miss Ferret and Miss Fields, who have moved from No. 32 Thornaugh-Street to No. 13 Cumberland Place. They have closed the Academy, and seem dissatisfied with their present position. They confirmed that Mary had lived with them six months, did not mention the reason for her going, and said that she had conducted herself to their satisfaction and been a very pleasant good servant.

Next I visited Mrs Mathews. I was particularly interested in meeting this good woman, for so much of Mary's story revolves around her. She is a most excellent woman, and thought of writing to you when she read of Mary's duplicity.

Mr Puttenden had been to St Giles Workhouse to pray with a sick woman and found Mary there. She was to be dismissed the next day. Finding her friendless, he had procured a place for her with Mrs Mathews.

Mary had lived with her for three years, during which time she suffered an illness. Mrs Mathews was very partial to her and said she was a capable, good servant, who seldom went out and never tippled. Mrs Mathews' daughter Betsey, who has since died, had taught Mary to read and write. Although her conduct was correct, she was rather eccentric and told terrible stories which, though they did no injury to others, Mrs Mathews feared were not good for her.

One of the things that Mary said was that she would like to live in the woods on her own, as a wild creature. Sometimes she would not eat for several days, to see how long she could live without food. Then one day she ran away suddenly on finding Mr Puttenden was coming to talk to her about some prank she had played.

Since leaving her service four years ago, Mary had returned to see Mrs Mathews several times. Once she called on her to ask for a good character for a gentleman from the Foundling Hospital was coming to see her, and if Mrs Mathews spoke well of Mary, her child would be admitted. The gentleman came, and the child was taken in.

In November 1816 they saw her for the last time. Her child was dead, she told them, and she was dressed in mourning. She told Mrs Mathews at this point that the child's father was a bricklayer.

Neither Mrs Mathews nor Mr Puttenden thought Mary had been abroad. It was not impossible, they told me, but extremely unlikely, although they had lost sight of her for some considerable time.

The same afternoon I visited Mrs Starling. Here I found the only record of Mary having behaved mischievously. One night she had set fire to two beds! In the course of one week she set fire to the same beds once more. The motive was, Mrs Starling thought, she did not like a fellow servant and wished HER to be suspected and dismissed.

Mrs Starling said she thought Mary did not mean to let the fire proceed to such a height that she could not extinguish it. Having played such a trick, Mrs Starling said, they could never again sleep in peace with Mary under their roof.

But – she still said Mary was the best servant she had ever had. She was odd and eccentric, and sometimes Mrs Starling wondered if she was right in her mind. She loved the children, but told them such strange stories about gypsies and werewolves she frightened them out of their wits.

Once she came into the parlour, dressed up like a gypsy, and the children did not know her. She told them she had been to the East Indies and America, that she had been brought to bed by the side of a river, and a lady and gentleman going by in a carriage had taken her up and adopted her as their daughter.

Such stories, Ma'am as we have heard in another guise.

She was with Mrs Starling when the child died, not at Miss Ferrett and Miss Fields as she stated. I believe Ma'am, she was ashamed of her stay there, and did not wish us to discover it. She made the mourning clothes there, and so quick, they were quite surprised when she put them on.

Mrs Starling said one day, having a talk with Mary in the kitchen, she thought she had discovered the story of Mary's seduction. In Mary's previous employment she had a chamber to herself, with no bolt on the door. Her Master let out lodgings to a foreign student, and it was this lad who surprised her, coming one night to her room where she lay naked in bed. He swore he loved her. She hoped – a foolish hope – that he might marry her. However, discovering she was pregnant he returned home without her. For a little while she heard from him, receiving money at intervals – then nothing. The money was sent to Mr Mitcham's of the Green Lion, Islington, and collected from thence. It came regularly for several months, and then stopped.

I wonder if Manuel Eynesso could be this man? It is too late to confront Mary with this, now, but perhaps he heard news of 'Caraboo' and recognised her from the description given in the newspapers and broadsheets. He would also have heard gossip about her.

I have been unable to trace this man. I wrote to the Marquis of X., in whose company he was when he visited Bristol, but my letter was returned unopened. He has left the country, a sick man, and is travelling in search of the sun. At his house they did not know when he would return.

Mrs Starling had read of Caraboo in the papers and knew at once that it was Mary. She thought of writing to you, but feared Mary might return and waylay Mr Starling on one of his walks home through the fields of Islington. I asked her, was Mary so very alarming? She replied No, but not to be relied upon, a prankster and unexpected, and Mr Starling was not a man of strong nerves.

I will next attend to the Magdalen, and then hope to return with all my errands done. I am most anxious to leave this plague pit of a city before the weather turns too hot.

Surely Mary cannot be 'right in the Head'? How can we discover the truth behind such an eccentric character? And yet she charms us all.

July 5th 1817
Today I visited the Magdalen Hospital. Here is the entry referring to her admittance. I copied it in my notebook word for word, as I am sure you would wish to read it.

STATED she was born November 11th 1792. That her parents were dead. That her father died when she was a month old. That he was a shoemaker in Witheridge in Devonshire. That her mother had been dead four years and a half. That her mother, on her deathbed, recommended her daughter to the protection of the Rev. Mr Luxham, Minister of Rechingford, near Witheridge. That he took her into his service, in which time she was seduced by a gentleman who visited the family. He took her to London, lived with her a month, then deserted her. After this she 'went on the town' and led a dissolute life. She had been in an Hospital two years previously.

Admitted under the Name ANNE BURGESS on February 4th 1813 and discharged at her own request July 22nd 1813.

After being at the Magdalen some weeks she said the account of herself was untrue, except that her father died in her infancy. Her name was not Burgess and no such gentleman as the Rev. Mr Luxham existed. She added that she had committed no misconduct and had assumed the name of Burgess.

I found out that during her stay at the Magdalen her conduct was very eccentric. She was restless and unsettled, but showed no propensity to vice. She did say, however, that she would hang herself, if it was discovered who she was.

On the 8th and 15th of July she asked for her discharge. She said she was not a fallen woman, and that she had been married. She would say no more.

But – Ma'am – the Matron said it was most odd. On the day after her discharge she called at the Magdalen again, not in the tattered clothes she had left the house wearing the previous day, but in clothes of a much better quality. She said she had left a box of clothes with a friend.

They heard no more of her until October 1814 when she called at the Magdalen Hospital, very decent in her dress, appearance and manners. She had walked to Exeter since having been at the Magdalen, and at Exeter she had found her former mistress, Mrs Partridge, and was going with her to France, as Cook.

The Matron told me she asked what Mrs Partridge had thought of Mary having been at the Magdalen.

'O,' Mary replied, 'she was well pleased, and said "I hope you will never forget the good advice you received there."'

I have computed the time that Mary lived with Mrs Mathews, and her other situations, and I cannot see that she had time to go abroad in service. The last eight years of her life are well accounted for, and her assertion that she has been in the East or in America are one of those unaccountable fictions for which she is well known.

To whom she was married, or who was the father of her child, remains a baffling mystery, along with some of the events of her life. It is impossible to ascertain the Truth.

I trust that you will not grieve too much over the fate of 'Caraboo' now that you will be able to understand the girl a little better. I pray that I have helped throw some light upon the matter, and have been of service to you.

I look forward with great anticipation to discussing the fruits of my labours on my return. You *may* be able to shed more light on my discoveries from your closeness to Mary over the past weeks.

I remain, Ma'am,
Your obed. humble svt.
J.C.M. Palmer

MRS WORRALL'S JOURNAL
JULY 21ST 1817

Captain Palmer has just been here, and we have been discussing C. and telling each other of her escapades and have made each other quite cheerful. I confess to being startled by the disclosures at Mrs Starling's – I had never dreamt that Mary would be so wild as to set fire to something; and indeed, Mrs Starling sounded quite afraid of her. Perhaps she did not treat her in quite the right way. Mary has always needed a firm hand, and then she shows the utmost admiration and respect.

Captain Palmer tells me there is a rumour, of course quite nonsense, that Mary was rowed to Elba from her ship, and met Napoleon, who proposed marriage! But as I told him, Elba is nowhere near Philadelphia, and she has barely left the shores of England. He agrees that the story is ridiculous, but for a time it made us laugh heartily.

Where is she now, I wonder?

I have heard no word of her. I cannot forget her, for I do truly miss her. I believe I never was so happy as in the brief few weeks in the Spring when she played the Princess for us all to applaud. I am convinced she is not entirely 'right in the head', as her Father says of her, for she BECOMES each part she plays, and believes in each story she tells.

My life here is so dull. Now.

Mr Worrall is deeply gloomy, for though the Bank has been printing notes, and seemed on the way to success, he says things are not going as well as he hoped. These matters of finance make my head ache. He says I must practise economy, and he will not continue with his wild gambling.

This must be the end of my Journal. I started to write it so that I would remember every detail of Caraboo, Princess of Javasu, in the hopes that it would one day be published, when we had discovered who she was, where she came from, and deciphered her language.

If I did not laugh, I would weep.

Mary Baker returned to England in 1820 and set herself up in Regent Street, Bristol, in a booth as 'The Princess Caraboo'. Few people came to see her. She had been forgotten.

APPENDICES

Letters to the papers

Letter from J.S.
to the Bath Chronicle

'It appears to have been Caraboo's intention to impersonate a French character. Before she left the confines of Bristol, passing through Park Row, she encountered two or three lace makers from Normandy who have established a manufactory in that part of the city. She watched their movements, and observed that everybody stared at them. This was food enough for her. She fixed her eyes on the French girls' head dress and it immediately occurred to her that in the guise of a foreigner she might obtain that which was denied to an Englishwoman. She soon twisted her handkerchief into a turban, outlandished her general attire, and set off on the Gloucestershire road. After walking a few miles a gentleman accosted her, and perceiving she was fatigued, took her to the next public house and gave her meat, spirits and water, which she, not being as yet a Hindoo, demolished à la Française, for she was now a French woman!'

An anonymous letter

'This girl was born at Witheridge, in Devonshire, in the year 1792, where her parents (poor but honest) are still living. Her mother taught her to spin wool, and obliged her to work as much as she could, but Mary evinced a strong inclination to follow the pursuits and habits of a boy. She therefore used to drive the farmer's horses, and when she was fatigued, would go into the water, and thus learned to swim and dive. Her mother being uneasy about her, procured her a place of service at Exeter, but she soon left it and commenced in earnest the life of a wandering mendicant . . . when she had expended all the money she collected on the road, she applied to "The Stranger's Friend Society" but an enquiry having been made into her character and history, she deemed it prudent to decamp, and set off for London. She procured a situation, as servant in a family, with whom she remained three years, but her mistress being very strict and refusing to allow her as much liberty as she wished, Mary packed up her little wardrobe and embraced the first opportunity of taking French leave. Being of an exceedingly romantic turn of mind, she now assumed male attire, and procured a place as a footman, and in this disguise she actually lived in her native place, close to her father's house, without exciting the smallest suspicion, having then acquired the art of altering her features so completely that no one knew her.

After residing in Witheridge some time she removed to a neighbouring village, but being sent with a message during the deep snow, she was overwhelmed and lay buried all night. In the morning she was found benumbed and insensible. The removal of her wet clothes discovered her sex and she was obliged to leave the place and set off on new adventures. Having begged her way to London, she again went into service, and again in a few months became weary of restraint and resumed her wandering habits of life. She now met with a foreigner, who, smitten with her charms, married her, and they travelled together to Brighton and other places on the South Coast. But the silken bonds of marriage became irksome to Mary and one morning she gave her sleeping husband the slip, retraced her steps to the metropolis, and again got into service.'

Letter from F.H.C.

'I well recollect the imposture of the Princess Caraboo in Bristol. My father was mainly instrumental in her detection. As a linguist he had been invited to pay her a visit, with a view to ascertaining what language she spoke. When he entered the room some gentleman had just placed before her an Oriental M.S. making signs to her to read it. She at once began to read it with great apparent facility, and aloud. My father observed quietly to a gentleman near him, out loud enough to be heard by Caraboo, that the language of the M.S. was read, like Hebrew, from right to left. In a few minutes she had changed her mode of pretending to read, and now traced the words from right to left. This opened the eyes of those in the room to her imposition, and she was soon forced to own it. She afterwards said that when she saw my father enter the room she dreaded him. He was persuaded from the first that she was an imposter, and probably his countenance indicated such persuasion.'

Bristoliensis, Notes and Queries

'I became acquainted with her in Bristol in December, 1849, when, after much reluctance, she gave me her signature "Mary Baker". She then lived under Pyle Hill, Bedminster, and gained her livelihood as well as supported her daughter by selling leeches to our infirmary hospital and to many of our druggists.

She avoided as much as possible any mention of her former career, of which I think she was ashamed; and nothing annoyed her more than when a neighbour's child ventured to call out after her, "CARABOO."

She died in December last year, but I have not yet been able to ascertain the exact date.'

The Times

'Such of our readers as are interested in the history of imposters will remember many years since a person who styled herself the "Princess Caraboo", and created a sensation in literary and fashionable circles of Bath and other places, which lasted till it was discovered the whole affair was a romance, cleverly sustained and acted out by a young and prepossessing girl. On being deposed from the honour accorded to her, the "princess" accepted the situation, retired into a comparatively humble life, and married. There was a kind of grim humour in the occupation which she subsequently followed – that of importer of leeches; but she conducted her operations with much judgement and ability, and carried on her trade with credit to herself, and satisfaction to her customers. The quondam "Princess" died recently in Bristol, leaving a daughter, who, like her mother, is said to be possessed of considerable personal attractions.'

Bristoliensis, Notes and Queries

'This remarkable woman was born November 11, 1792, at Witheridge, Devonshire, and was the second child of Thomas Willcocks, an honest hardworking man, by trade a cobbler, and of Mary, his wife. This daughter was named Mary, and was admitted to the Magdalen hospital, London, under the feigned name of Anne Burgess, on February 4th, 1813, previously to which she had led a loose life for some years. One of the men with whom she cohabited and to whom she stated she was married after two months acquaintance, by a Romish priest, was a foreigner from whom doubtless she learned the Malay language and thus became acquainted with Asiatic customs and idioms.'

Notes

SAMUEL WORRALL

'On January 18th 1808 the Bristol Tolzey Bank opened in Corn Street, Bristol. The partners in this concern were Samuel Worrall, Andrew Pope and John Edmonds. Samuel Worrall was the senior partner. He was the eldest son of Samuel Worrall, who was also a Banker. He married Elizabeth, by whom he had two sons. He was a stamp distributor for the city, was educated a barrister, and was appointed Town Clerk in 1787, remaining in that office until 1819, the year the Bank failed. In consideration of his services for thirty-two years, the Council ordered the sum of £400 to be paid annually to the Mayor and Alderman in trust for the use of the Town Clerk and of his wife and family for the rest of his life.

'He was nicknamed "Devil Worrall" and the three partners were called the Devil, the Pope (Andrew Pope) and the Pretender (a stranger to the city, called John Edmonds).'

Charles Henry Cave, *History of Banking in Bristol* (1899)

In 1819 there is a note in *Latimer's Annals of Bristol* referring to the failure of the Bank.

'Great consternation was caused in the city and neighbourhood by the failure of the Tolzey Bank. Though of recent origin the Bank had issued a great number of notes for twenty shillings and thirty shillings each, and the disaster affected all classes in the locality, causing a 'run' upon several of the other Banks, then eleven in number.'

Samuel Worrall was obliged to resign his office a few days later, on being declared a bankrupt.

Newsman's verses, 1819:

> 'Of all the things within the year
> that made our market place to stare
> Not one more rare and strange to say:
> Than 'Tolzey Bank – no longer pay:
> And all the paper with the cross*
> Be little better than a loss.'

'Samuel Worrall died in November, 1821. In his prosperous days he was a man of great entertaining powers in convivial society, which led to his introduction to the Prince Regent, and he was a frequent guest at Carlton House. On the other hand, he was rude and coarse to his inferiors, and gained in some way the nickname "Devil Worrall" of which he seemed proud.

He lived for many years in a house opposite the Council House, and on one occasion, upon coming home from a party a little "elevated", as he was getting out of the hackney coach his foot slipped, and he fell to the ground. A crowd immediately assembled, and amongst them a very harmless and quiet silk mercer who resided in the High Street, under the name of Camplin. Worrall, still on his back, fixed his eyes on the unfortunate mercer and pointing at him, said "that's the man that knocked me down," upon which the crowd took part with the town clerk, and poor Camplin was obliged to run, protesting his innocence.

To fully realise this scene, it must be remembered that the bibulous official presided on the magisterial bench at every quarter sessions.'

ELIZABETH WORRALL

After Samuel Worrall's death Elizabeth Worrall moved to Clifton, where she lived at No. 4 Beaufort Buildings. A few years later she moved to 7 The Pentagon, Clifton, where she lived from 1828 to her death in 1842 at the age of 75. She appears to have been tolerably well off, for she employed two female servants, Jane and another Elizabeth.

Mrs Worrall had two sons, one of whom became a general in the Bengal Cavalry. He lived at 20 Caledonia Place and had three children, Sophia, Jessie and Edith, so Mrs Worrall had much to occupy her.

In the Cathedral there is a monumental inscription in memory of 'Georgina Lucy Worrall who died 10th February 1832, aged four years and 7 months, erected by her grandmother, Elizabeth Worrall.'

---

* A picture of the Bristol High Cross was engraved on the notes of the Tolzey.

There is a Worrall Road in Clifton, Bristol.

It would be fascinating to know whether Mrs Worrall saw Mary when she returned to England and set herself up as an 'Exhibition' in Bond Street, Bath. 'See the Princess Caraboo of Javasu! Visit the Famous Imposter!' I wonder if she did?

ST PETER'S HOSPITAL, THE WORKHOUSE, BRISTOL

The building was constructed first in 1401 by Thomas and Walter Norton. Thomas Norton was reputed to have discovered the elixir of life, but the advantages of this appear to have escaped him. Robert Aldworth, a merchant, reconstructed the building in 1601.

After the Aldworths, the building served as a sugar house, and a refinery was set up there. Later it became the branch Mint of the City of Bristol.

In 1698 it was purchased for £800 by the Corporation of the City of Bristol and became the Workhouse and Infirmary. The Court room had been the drawing room of the Aldworths, and was fitted up as a Board or Meeting room for the Guardians of the Poor.

In the early days of the Poor Law administration, a subterranean cell at the rear of the building was fitted as a workroom where the inmates dressed flax. This spot was called Purgatory. Stocks and a whipping post were installed as a means of punishment.

The general procedure during the early nineteenth century was to make the Workhouse as unpleasant as possible, to avoid the drain on the Poor Rates. All possessions were taken from the inmates, and they were dressed alike in coarse, rough clothes. Food was generally bad. The rules of the Poor Law Board were usually hung up in dining halls, wards, and nurseries. These related punishments for Disorderly and Refractory Paupers, listing various forms of offences such as 'Obscene and Profane Language, playing at Cards, Climbing over Fences and Boundary walls, violence and insubordination of any kind.'

One trained Matron and a staff of untrained pauper nurses who were given food and lodgings but no pay, generally ran the Workhouse. The Matron was supposed to visit each ward every day. She controlled every department, and was answerable only to the Guardians. The respectable poor lived in dread of the visit of the Parish officers, who insulted them by speaking harshly to them, as though to criminals. Indeed, in many cases the Workhouse was seen as being a worse place than prison.

There were weekly visits by Men Guardians of the Poor. In 1857 the first Women Guardians were admitted. This was so that the women inmates would have a fellow female to whom to complain; but on the walls of every room was a printed notice stating that all complaints must be made in writing to the Master, and by him presented to the Lady Guardians. These complaints were entered into a book for all to see. Thus the inmates were afraid to complain.

In the 1800s there were 500 pauper nurses in London. One half of these were above 50, one quarter above 60, many not less than 70 years of age, and some more than 80.

In 1772 a booklet listing Charitable Institutions in Bristol states:

St Peters, Peter Street is the General Hospital for the Poor of the Whole City including superannuated Persons, Orphans, and Ideots [sic] and has a ward for Lunatics. Vagrants, and Beggars, are taken up and sent thither. It is supported by an annual assessment on housekeepers, and conducted by the following gentlemen:

Here follows a list of names, with the Matron the only woman. By 1830 the trade of the country was so depressed, states *Latimer's Annals of Bristol* (1887), and St Peter's Hospital was so over full that the Corporation of the Poor was plunged into acute embarrassment. The building was 'gorged with 600 inmates, in a most unhealthy condition, as well as a sink of moral contamination. Fifty-eight girls slept in 10 beds and eighty boys in seventeen beds. Just at this time an epidemic of cholera reached the city, and it is not surprising to learn that the malady nowhere worked more dreadful havoc than in the Workhouse. In fact, out of the first 261 cases reported in the city, 168 occurred in St Peter's Hospital.'

New buildings were bought to house the inmates, and the 'Hospital', no longer a workhouse, was burnt to the ground in the blitz of 1940.

THE ENCLOSURE ACTS

Before 1700 England consisted of great tracts of open fields, divided into strips and farmed by the men of the village nearby. Everyone in the village was expected to help, and as a result the village was largely self-supporting. Around the village was a 'waste' or common land, where the villagers could pasture their cattle, sheep, pigs or geese, with the right to firewood, berries, nuts or fruit in season.

From 1700 onwards this way of life ceased in most villages. The land began to be enclosed by Act of Parliament, for the benefit of landowners and rich farmers, in order to make more economic use of the land.

By 1760 there were 2,500 Enclosure Acts, incorporating some four million acres of open fields. Another 1,800 Acts enclosed some two million acres of 'waste' or common land. In the time of the Napoleonic wars even Dartmoor and Exmoor were ploughed in parts.

This had the effect of pauperising whole villages, who now had to rely on being employed by the farmer and sending their children out to work.

FOUNDLING HOSPITAL

Thomas Coram, a shipbuilder who had made his fortune in New England, was so upset by seeing children dead or dying, exposed on the side of the road as he travelled from Rotherhythe, where he lived, to the Docks, where he worked, that he conceived the idea of setting up a Foundling Hospital for the reception of unwanted children.

He bought 56 acres in Lamb's Conduit Fields for £5,500 and by 1745 one wing of the building was completed. The hospital was a great success. It was granted a Royal Charter, and Hogarth, an early benefactor, presented three pictures to it. Handel gave the hospital an organ and the benefit of 'The Messiah', the performance of which he conducted himself. He bequeathed the property of the Oratorio to the hospital on his death.

At the time the building was ready to receive infants 'any person who brought a child was directed to come in at the outward door and ring a bell at the inward door, and not to depart until the child is returned (diseased children not admitted) or given notice of its reception'. Each child, it was hoped, should have a distinguishing mark or token by which it might afterwards be recognised. Most of these tokens were small coins, or parts of coins. Sometimes an old silk purse or doggerel verse was pinned to the child's garment, and once a lottery ticket.

The number of applicants was enormous. The outward door was besieged by women who fought and scratched their way to the bell on the inward door. The strongest won.

To stop this, babies were admitted by ballot.

After fifteen years the Governors had to apply to Parliament for assistance. This was given so liberally that nursing establishments were set up all over the country. A basket was hung up outside the hospital gate and an advertisement tendered stating that all children under the age of two months would be received. The result was that on June 2nd, 1756, the basket was filled and emptied 117 times. A new Carriers trade commenced. Baby Carriers undertook to convey infants to the basket from distant parts of the country. One mother followed the Carrier on foot to breast feed her baby the whole way down from Yorkshire. During the 3 years 10 months of the system, 15,000 children dropped in the basket.

Captain Coram died financially ruined, supported by subscription. 'He was often seen, clad in his well-worn red coat, seated on a bench under the Arcade, with tears in his eyes, regaling small Foundlings with gingerbread.'

By 1801 the rules of admission were as follows: The mother rang the bell and received a printed form of admission. Her child must be the first born, and preference given to cases 'in which deception was practised'. She must never have lived with the father. The idea behind this was the 'restoration of the mother into society.'

When the child was admitted a wet nurse was summoned from a nursing district in Kent and the child was taken to the chapel to be baptized. Here, at the altar, awaited the Matron, Steward, Schoolmaster, and Head Nurse. Names were a difficulty. The first 20 had, at their baptism, 'a fine appearance of persons of quality. His Grace the Duke of Bedford, their Graces the Duke and Duchess of Richmond, the Countess of Pembroke . . . all honouring the children with their names and being sponsors.' Many of the foundlings grew up and embarrassed their sponsors by claiming kinship. When the peerage was exhausted, historical celebrities were adopted, then characters from novels, then the Governors used their own names.

The babies were taken to Kent with their wet nurses, each of whom gave a receipt for the child. They received a little packet of clothes and a document which stated the terms and conditions under which the child was to be reared. 25/- would be paid at the end of the first year as a gratuity on top of board and lodging.

By 1815 there were 195 boys and girls in the Foundling Hospital and 180 boys and girls in Kent. When they were old enough to walk they came back to the Hospital to be schooled, and at 14 they were dismissed and apprenticed to trades or places.

The Rules of Admission for Mary would have been as follows: 'Women whose infants are proper objects of the Foundling Charity and not above a year old, may apply on any Wednesday, before ten-o-clock, to the Secretary at the Hospital, with petitions, which may be prepared by themselves, if they can write, if not, by a friend.'

R.H. Nichols and Wray, *Foundling Hospital* (OUP 1935)
Ackerman Microcosm of London (1808)

POOR LAWS

Latimer's Annals

The punishment of whipping appears to have been still highly approved by the local justices, and continued so for several years. *The Bristol Journal* of December 4th 1819, contained the following: 'A man who has been loitering about our city for some days, and who was taken to the Council-house charged with being a nuisance, was publicly whipped on Tuesday at the pump in Wine Street, and immediately after passed to his parish. We cannot too highly applaud the conduct of the Magistrates.' Sometimes the crowds had their pockets picked during the 'exhibition'.

The Speenhamland system

In May 1795, Berkshire magistrates decided that a dole from the Poor Rate in each parish would supplement a man's wages, depending on the price of bread and the number of children he had. This idea rapidly became law and was supported by Parliament. In effect, the large farmer benefited because he did not raise wages, and the small farmer's rates increased. The labourer became a pauper. A single man with no family could not draw the dole. The farming boom of the Napoleonic war years disguised the problem of rural poverty for a time. In 1815 peace brought depression. 250,000 men from the Army and Navy came back from the war looking for jobs. In 1815 the Corn Law, prohibiting corn imports, made bread dearer. In 1816 there were riots in Suffolk. Crime figures swelled. Game laws became harsher. By the 1820s William Cobbett, in *Rural Rides*, has this to say, 'What injustice, what a hellish system it must be, to make those who raise it [food] skin and bone and nakedness, while the food and drink are almost all carried away to be heaped on swarms of tax eaters.'

'Sophia Edwards and Mary West, two female servants of the Rev. John Gibbons, of Brasted, Kent (one aged 22 and the other 19 years), were found drowned in a pond in the garden belonging to the Parsonage-house of that place; and the same day an inquest was taken on their bodies when the following circumstances were disclosed: Mr and Mrs Gibbons had been from home several weeks, leaving their house to the care of these females, who, during the absence of their master and mistress, had the misfortune to break some articles of furniture, and to spoil four dozen of knives and forks, by incautiously lighting a fire in an oven where they had been placed to keep them from rust. The unfortunate girls had, however, bought other knives and forks.

Upon the return of Mr and Mrs Gibbons (on Sunday, the 14th) the servants were severely reprimanded for what had happened, and one of them received notice to leave her place. They both appeared very uncomfortable during Sunday and Monday, and on the latter day the footman heard them conversing respecting Martha Viner, a late servant IN THE SAME FAMILY who had drowned herself in a pond in the garden, and observing one to the other, that she had done so through trouble.

The elder one then said to the younger, "We will have a swim tonight, Mary!" The other replied, "So we will, girl." The footman thought they were jesting, and said "Aye, and I will swim with you." Sophia Edwards replied, "No you shan't. But I will have a swim, and afterwards I will haunt you." After this conversation they continued their work as usual, and at six o'clock asked the footman to get tea for them; while he was in the pantry for that purpose, he heard the kitchen door shut, and on his return to the kitchen they were both gone. The footman afterwards thought he heard them upstairs, and therefore took no notice of their absence until eight o'clock, when he told his master and mistress.

Search was made for them about the house, garden, and neighbourhood, during the whole night; and early on Tuesday morning the same pond was dragged which had so recently been the watery grave of Martha Viner, when both their bodies were found in it, lying close to each other.

The jury returned the verdict of "found drowned".'

The Annual Register (November, 1812)

THE MAGDALEN

The Magdalen was one of the first of the charities in the new Humanitarian movement, having been started by Robert Dingley, a Dilettante (see p 206), in 1758, helped by Jonas Hanway and others.

The committee convened every Thursday and interviewed each applicant, for the simple reason that penniless girls with nowhere to go would try every means in their power to enter the Magdalen, but until they became prostitutes they were unable to do so.

The Magdalen usually housed 112 young women, and the Magdalens stayed two years in the hospital, in three successive wards. Probationary, the first, lasted only a short time if the behaviour was good. Then the inmate went into one of six intermediate wards, with fourteen other women, and lastly finished her stay in one of two finishing wards.

The inmates had one warm bath a week, and morning and evening washing. They had separate cubicles in the dormitory, with a bed and a washstand in each, and they were issued with Sunday clothes as well as the regulation workday clothes; a best dress of light brown with a white tippet folded across the bosom, and a white cap worn forward over the forehead. They also had a warm shawl for cold weather.

The food was excellent. Roast beef and puddings are mentioned for Sunday lunch, or boiled mutton, or mutton broth and rice. They ate bread when it was not too dear, and were given half a pound of meat daily with half a pint of milk and two and a half pints of beer. They often complained the beer was watered, for the Magdalen brewed its own beer and for a time kept it in a loft above the Chapel.

The girls worked at all manner of things; making and mending linen, making lace, artificial flowers and children's toys, cauls, ladies shoes, millinery, stays, weaving hair for wigs, knitting hose and mittens, and sewing garters. They received money for their work, and were able to set aside a small sum for when they left the hospital.

In their final period the Magdalens learnt cooking, scullery work, house cleaning and waiting at table.

One of the chief attractions of the Magdalen was the Chapel, to which society flocked. The penitents sang so beautifully, and looked so angelic that the young men about town would mark one out to proposition on her return to the outside world. There was such a crush to get into the Chapel that bribery was used to obtain tickets.

When built in St George's Field (Blackfriars), the Magdalen had been literally in the fields; but when Mary was there slum buildings had edged right up to the walls of the hospital, and prostitution flourished under the windows. A theatre called 'Hughes Riding School', later known as the 'Surrey Theatre', was close by and sometimes the Magdalens were called by name from the streets outside. From the upper windows of the theatre people could look down into the wards, so the windows had to be blocked up and a skylight substituted. The language was so awful, floating up from the streets, that the nursery windows had to be kept shut at night, and no lady visitors could possibly sleep in the spare room.

H.F.B. Compston, *The Magdalen Hospital* (1917)

THE REFECTORY

' . . . where all the nuns, without their hats, were ranged at long tables, ready for supper. A few were handsome, many who seemed to have no title to their profession, and two or three of twelve years old: but all recovered and looking healthy. I was struck and pleased by the modesty of two of them, who swooned away with the confusion of being stared at: one of them is the niece of Sir Clement Cotterel. We

were shown their work: which is making linen and bead work, they earn £10 a
week . . .'

Sir Horace Walpole (1760)

DILETTANTE

Horace Walpole said that the qualifications for membership of the Dilettante were
'drunkenness and a tour of Italy.'

Robert Dingley was a philanthropist and merchant; Jonas Hanway was noted for
being the first man to carry an umbrella through the streets of London, being hooted
at by errand boys and meeting ridicule and sneers from sedan chair carriers. He was
always cold and dressed in three pairs of stockings on the hottest day. He was a total
abstainer from tea, which he considered as dangerous to the health as gin, and he
directly attributed Samuel Johnson's shaking hands, as he spilled tea over his
breeches, to the effect of tea poisoning. Jonas Hanway fought tooth and nail against
the washerwomen at the Magdalen Laundry being allowed tea to drink instead of
beer, but he was finally defeated in 1762.

CHARLES HUNNINGS WILKINSON MRCS (1763/4–1850)

Charles Hunnings Wilkinson, a colourful eccentric, lectured extensively on galvan-
ism and was a pioneer in medical electricity. On the title page of *Elements of
Galvanism*, his most significant published work (1804, dedicated to Sir Joseph
Banks) he is described as a Member of the Royal College of Surgeons and of the
Philosophical Society of Manchester, Associate of the Institute of Medicine in Paris,
Lecturer in Experimental Philosophy to the City Institution, Honorary Member of
the Physical Societies of Guy's, Bartholomews, the Lyceum *Medicum Londinense*, and
of the London Philosophical and Mathematical Societies. His lectures on Experimental Philosophy at Bart's covered mechanics, optics, electricity, magnetism, astronomy,
etc. The doctor was said to 'go into everything, nothing was above or beneath his
grasp; it was amazing to hear him theorize upon every new invention, and dogmatize
upon every conceivable topic'.

He wrote a number of books, largely for self advertisement, but also to explain his
new inventions.

As a cure for wheezing, asthma, difficulties of breathing, and pains in the chest,
Dr Wilkinson experimented with inhaling Rock Oil or Green Mineral Naptha from
Barbados (also called Coal Oil).

The patient inhaled the fumes from a vessel of Dr Wilkinson's construction. This
'resembled a coffee pot, a tube issuing from the top, with a corresponding opening
on the opposite side to allow a draft [sic], so that the vapour may ascend. The iron
is what may be obtained at any ironmongers; laundresses use it for what they term
the Italian iron. This heater being attached to a firm rod, terminating in a wooden

handle, is altogether 18 foot in length. The cover or lid of the pot is made to slide on this rod so that when the heater is made hot, upon being immersed in the tar, the cover fits on, and prevents any escape of vapour. The tube of the pot is then kept to the nostril, at the proper distance, that the vapour may be inspired [sic]. Care must be taken that the heater be not red hot, in which case ignition of the gases, attended by an explosion, will happen, and may be of serious consequence. This happened once with me; I therefore caution those who use the remedy, to observe the degree of heat ere the heater be immersed in the tar; neglect of this observance on my part occasioned ignition and burnt the eyelashes and eyebrows of my little patient, Walles.'

Patients were offered portable electric machines for use in their own homes. These could treat affections of the head, tooth and ear ache, deafness, paralysis, asthma and impotence.

In 1811 he was living in Bath, where he leased the King's or Roman Bath (two ladies in one Bath, 3/6). He gave lectures on Chemistry and Mineralogy, and he wrote a treatise on the properties of the Bath waters. In a book on Naptha he claimed to have introduced Bi-carbonate of soda as a cure for dyspepsia. Although he began to use the initials MD after his name, it is doubtful whether he ever qualified in Britain other than as MRCS.

He became proprietor of the Pump Room and a well known figure in Bath. Owing to his linguistic abilities he was called upon to meet Caraboo, and his enthusiasm for her cause, resulting in her disclosure, earned him the nickname of 'Dr Caraboo'.

In later life he lived at No. 55 Pulteney Street, Bath. In an appendix to one of his publications he has turned his attentions to 'the physiological enquiries into the structure of the Enunciation Organs. NB Any Person thus afflicted, by stating every particular (post paid) to the Author, will preclude the necessity of personal attendance.'

He died 'deeply regretted' states the *Bath Herald*, at the ripe old age of eighty-seven.

From: J.L. Thornton *Annals of Science Dec.* 1967
Dr C.H. Wilkinson. *Annals of Science* 1798
Dr C.H. Wilkinson. Pamphlet. Bath 1830